How to have a
QUALITY LIFE

Martin Raj

© 2024 Martin Raj

All rights reserved. No portion of this book may be reproduced, stored in a retrieval system, or transmitted in any form or by any means--electronic, mechanical, photocopy, recording, scanning, or other--except for brief quotations in critical reviews or articles, without the prior written permission of the publisher.

All the stories related in this book are true, but most of the names have been changed to protect the privacy of the people mentioned.

Scripture taken from the New King James Version®. Copyright © 1982 by Thomas Nelson. Used by permission. All rights reserved.

Edited by Sabrina Petersen
Book cover design and layout by Lokesh Richards

This book is dedicated with love to
my mummu, G. Ruby Ravi Kumari.

You have sincerely prayed for me and Ivan anna.
Your prayers of protection and blessings are still felt
even though you are not with us. I know that one day,
when we all go to heaven,
you will get to read this book.
Until then, I will miss you!

Disclaimer

This book is for educational purposes only and is not intended to diagnose, treat, cure, or prevent any medical or psychological condition. The content focuses on mindset and spirituality to provide insights and encouragement for personal growth. It should not replace professional advice, diagnosis, or treatment. Always seek the guidance of a qualified healthcare provider with any questions you may have regarding your mental health or medical condition.

ACKNOWLEDGEMENTS

With special thanks:

To my dear wife, Debbie Raj, for recommending claiming each fruit of the Spirit during our prayers, which inspired me to write this book. I appreciate the time you spent reviewing this book, giving your honest input and suggestions, being my biggest cheerleader, and most of all, praying for me and with me while writing. Your dedication to our family and your irreplaceable love is highly treasured.

To my beloved brother, Ivan Raj, who has been a moral support throughout this journey. Your constant inquiries, appreciation of my work, and belief in what God has placed in my heart have been invaluable.

To my adopted parents, Queen and George Foster, for your care and encouragement. You have taught me more about God's love and how one can bless others even without sharing the same blood.

To my in-laws, Billy, Rosemarie, and Christian, since the moment you learned about this book, your excitement has been unmatched. Your continued appreciation, eagerness to hear parts from the book, and encouragement in helping me finish this project are truly appreciated.

To all my Chiloquin Church family, for your unparalleled support. I appreciate each one of you for showing interest in this book and for giving me numerous opportunities to speak from its contents. You all are dear to my heart.

To all my dearest friends who have been praying throughout this process and all those who helped make this book a reality. I want to express my deepest gratitude to you all and know that your support means the world to me.

What people say about Quality Life:

In a world where thousands are going through life without any meaning, purpose and happiness, the book "How to Have a Quality Life" is an excellent and insightful resource for those desiring to experience fulfillment in life. This work departs from man-made standards of happiness to a God-centered approach as to what constitutes real value in life, which thousands sadly ignore today. In a simple, yet captivating way, the author outlines, in a very creative manner, the nine fruits of the Spirit found in the Bible through inspiring personal stories, illustrations and Biblical principles, as the keys to achieve such a quality life.

–Daniel Miranda, Pastor,
Orosi-Sanger Bilingual SDA Churches

In a world that draws upon our carnal nature and encourages us to walk in the flesh, Martin Raj has given us a volume that encourages us to walk in the Spirit and exude His fruit. Martin has managed to strike the balance between holistic health and spirituality and this is needed in our world. Lastly, the book seamlessly blends simplicity and profundity and the real life stories keep you engaged from start to finish. If you want a balanced holistic lifestyle, How to Have a Quality Life is the book for you.

–Simdumise Poswa, Pastor,
Central Peninsula 2 District, Cape Town

Martin Raj has crafted this book to help readers understand how to acquire a QUALITY LIFE through a change in their approach to daily life's incidents. This change helps in building character. This book is a must-read for anyone who needs a "push" to overcome negativity and discouragement and access various blessings. In a world full of darkness and gloom, this book is sure to make a positive change in your life!

–Ivan Raj,
Founder of The Wisdom Pearl

Table of Contents

Foreword 1

Introduction 3

Chapter 1 - Joy: Experiencing Lasting Joy 11

Chapter 2 - Peace: Are You A Hoarder? 29

Chapter 3 - Patience: Finding Purpose In Waiting..............47

Chapter 4 - Kindness: Developing A Gentle Spirit 69

Chapter 5 - Virtue: Essence of Time Well Spent 81

Chapter 6 - Humility: Who Is In Control? 99

Chapter 7 - Value: Did You Find Your Worth Yet?...........109

Chapter 8 - Faith: Something We All Possess....................135

Chapter 9 - Love: What Is Love? 165

Conclusion..189

FOREWORD

I have had the privilege and blessing of knowing Martin for the last seven years. We met at a vegan cafe and bonded over a shared excitement for ministering to the whole person—believing that health is a beautiful combination of the physical, emotional, mental, and spiritual.

Over the following months, I came to know him more deeply as he shared his story. He and his brother Ivan were raised in India by a single mother under very trying circumstances. Their mother was a deeply committed Christian who prayed often and believed in and experienced the power of Jesus Christ personally. Sadly, she suffered from multiple organ failure in the last years of her life. During those difficult times, she shared with Martin and Ivan her strong conviction of God's purpose for their lives. She believed that God had created Martin to study and learn God's healing principles. This was a great challenge for Martin, as he had other ideas and was already successfully employed in secular business. But through a series of providential miracles, Martin found himself studying natural healing at a small school in Africa.

From there, he came to America and enrolled in an excellent four-year program to learn how to combine spiritual with practical physical and emotional healing. He learned how to cooperate with God as he worked with his clients to bring relief from physical pain through massage, nutrition, and lifestyle changes. This opened up the hearts of those he was working with, allowing them to experience the peace and purpose they were seeking in their lives.

We worked together at that vegan cafe for a year and a half. I retired, but we stayed in touch. God led him to his beautiful wife Debbie and to more opportunities to practice the healing principles of the Bible.

In the providence of God, Martin has been inspired to write this book, "How To Have Quality Life." In it, he has structured his teaching around the beautiful fruit of the Holy Spirit as spoken about in Galatians 5:22-23. His personal experiences of joy, peace, long-suffering, kindness, goodness, humility, temperance, faith, and, most importantly, unselfish and self-sacrificing love are both inspiring and refreshing. His development of each theme with interesting and enlightening experiences that others have had makes the pathway to developing a quality life clear and attainable for all.

I believe you will be inspired and blessed as you read about how to enjoy the greatest fulfillment of a genuine and meaningful life. "For it is God who works in you both to will and to do of His good pleasure." (Philippians 2:13)

—Pastor Rick Kuntz

INTRODUCTION

As Jeannie powered through her workout on the elliptical at the gym, a stranger approached her.

"Could I ask you a question?" the stranger inquired.

Jeannie flashed a friendly smile. "Sure!"

The stranger hesitated before blurting out, "Well, somebody told me you were 85."

Jeannie's eyes twinkled with amusement. "They did?" she quipped, keeping her tone light.

With a nervous chuckle, the stranger admitted, "Yes! Hope I didn't offend you!"

Jeannie brushed off the concern with a dismissive wave of her hand. "No, not at all. I am 87," she clarified, still grinning.

The stranger's curiosity had been piqued. "Could I take a picture of you?"

Jeannie's laughter filled the air as she agreed, intrigued by the stranger's request. "Of course," she replied.

As the stranger snapped the picture, she revealed her motive. "I want to show this to my mother. She's 75 and won't get off the couch."

A couple years later, when I asked Jeannie what she would consider to be a quality life, her answer was the following:

- Having God in one's life. She acknowledged that, like everyone else, she has faced trials and struggles, but having God with her has made all the difference.
- Being forgiven. Despite making mistakes along the way, Jeannie finds comfort in knowing that God has forgiven her.
- Maintaining a positive attitude towards life. Life brings both good and bad experiences, but how we approach them matters.
- Surrounding yourself with positive people and avoiding negative influences that can bring you down.
- Building a community to support and uplift each other. She believes that we can learn from each other and grow together.
- Keeping oneself healthy by maintaining a disciplined exercise routine.

As she reflected on her 91 years of life, she described it as a great adventure filled with ups and downs and good friendships. She truly believes she's had a quality life.

Just like Jeannie, everyone is in pursuit of a quality life. However, many create lifestyle patterns based on external influences, such as relationships, social status, educational status, acts of charity, religious practices, partying, unrestrained sexual behavior, pursuing wealth, etc.

Some people understand that their quality of life depends on internal influences, so they try different lifestyle practices, such as worship, meditation, yoga, or martial arts.

But what is a QUALITY LIFE? How does one achieve it? Is it achieved through external influences or internal influences? Defining quality of life is tricky. The assumption is that it differs from person to person and may fluctuate from time to time. While one might find something helpful in achieving a quality life, someone else might find something completely different to help achieve their quality life.

If you had asked me that question when I was in my teen years, my answer would have been being rich, and my brother's answer would have been being taller. If you ask a forty-year-old single, their answer might be being married. If you ask a forty-year-old married couple, their answer might be not being married. A rich person's definition might be having peace, a sick person's might be health, and the list goes on. However, I want you to think about this with me.

When we say, "This is a quality product" or "Those are quality foods," or we talk about spending "quality time" with family, we are always referring to something that is excellent, superior, higher, or better than the norm. The word *quality* typically has a positive connotation unless it is followed by the words *poor* or *low*.

> *"Something doesn't lose its quality based on an individual's opinion."*

What makes something quality better than the rest? Quality products are not made by chance. Quality foods are not prepared by chance. Quality time with family doesn't happen by chance. There is a deliberate effort made to add special value to these things—and anything considered quality, for that matter. It's interesting to note that something doesn't lose its quality based on an individual's opinion. Even if someone doesn't personally like a product, food, or activity, the value remains unchanged. This means that certain products are objectively superior to other products, regardless of an individual's opinion.

For example, you can certainly see the difference between $100 headphones and $10 headphones. Similarly, certain foods are objectively higher quality than others, such as those served at a five Michelin star restaurant compared to a fast-food chain. Additionally, certain uses of time are more valuable than others. Intentionally spending a couple hours every day with the family is much more valuable than simply sleeping eight hours in the same house with them every day.

Now that we have clarified the definition of quality, let's understand what quality of life entails.

Although the perception of a quality life may seem subjective, there are nine key components essential for each individual to experience it fully: joy, peace, patience, kindness, virtue, humility, temperance, faith, and love. As these elements form the foundation of our lives, a quality life ensues.

From our early stages of life, we seek out our identity, life purpose, and true love. Unfortunately, in most cases, the identity, purpose, and love we acquire end up being counterfeit, providing only short-term or temporary fulfillment and leaving us depleted, searching for more, and feeling dissatisfied with our lives. Consequently, we find ourselves chasing after one method or another to discover our true identity, purpose, and love, or we just settle for a mediocre life. These nine key components will not only help you cease the cycle of chasing but will also guide you towards a fulfilled life in the long term. They will aid you in uncovering your true identity, purpose, and love. By integrating these components internally, they will be reflected outwardly. This holistic approach will provide you with a purposeful life filled with love and contentment.

Though judgments or opinions from others may fluctuate, your quality of life will remain steadfast. It won't be easily shaken like leaves of autumn but rather will resemble a firmly rooted tree in the earth.

These nine key components serve as the main chapters and foundational themes or guiding principles of this book. They provide a comprehensive framework for living a fulfilling and enriched life.

Living a quality life is a skill, and it doesn't happen automatically or by chance. Just like anything else, this kind of life must be developed meticulously with the right attitude. Let's consider a car as an analogy: while it consists of tens of thousands of parts, there are a few basic components that are necessary for the car to start, move, and come to a complete stop. With one of these basic components missing, the car won't start. However, even with these basic components, two vital factors are required for the vehicle to operate.

The first one is fuel. While it's not part of the vehicle itself, fuel is indispensable for its function. Similarly, if one desires a fulfilling life, the nine components mentioned earlier are crucial. Yet, there is one that is indispensable—like fuel—to get these nine to work. As you read through the chapters, you'll identify what components you are lacking and how to include them in your daily life to experience quality of life. You'll also learn about the indispensable factor that will make these key components part of your life.

The second factor is vital for the car to function as well. Did you guess it yet? Yes, you got it! It's the driver. Even with all the key components and the indispensable fuel, the car won't start or move by itself. When it comes to a quality life, the driver is the attitude of commitment. It is these that give you the drive to achieve quality of life to its fullest.

Take these stories as inspiration for how commitment can help develop the nine key components of a quality life:

Story# 1

The late Mr. Paul was an 88-year-old friend whom I used to take on walks once in a while. As a life coach, I tried to help him with his body posture because he had bowed legs and postural hyperkyphosis caused by old age. (Hyperkyphosis is an exaggerated curvature of the spine.) During one of our walks, I discovered that he had been married to his wife (who had passed away a few years prior to this conversation) for over sixty years. I was astonished.

Upon learning this, I couldn't help but ask him, "What is the secret to staying together for so long?"

His answer was simple yet profound: "We loved each other. While we faced some challenges initially, we worked through them, and we rarely had any major issues."

His response was accompanied by a broad smile, revealing his deep love for his late wife and the void her absence had left in his life.

As I reflect on my time with him, I realize he could have easily spoken negatively about his wife since she had passed away, and no one else was with us to challenge his words. However, not once did he utter a negative remark about his wife; instead, he always expressed his admiration for her and spoke of how much he missed her. Their marriage was a testament to their unwavering commitment, resulting in a beautiful quality of life together.

Story# 2

Drib came as a health guest to the wellness center where my wife and I worked, seeking assistance with his second-stage prostate cancer. Despite his diagnosis, I noticed his remarkably positive attitude and willingness to make the necessary changes for his health. Following the conclusion of the eleven-day program, he returned home, but I observed through his Facebook updates that he remained dedicated to his exercise routine, maintained a healthy diet, and continued implementing what he had learned at the wellness center.

Nearly a year later, Drib returned to the center to pick up his sister, and he shared an incredible update. He revealed that a few months after completing the program, he visited his doctor to check on his prostate cancer. To his amazement, the doctor informed him that there was no evidence of cancer. However, the doctor recommended seeking a second opinion, which Drib did. The second doctor confirmed the initial diagnosis—there was no sign of cancer.

"Today's commitment is tomorrow's achievement!"

Drib's commitment to his health played a significant role in his journey to being cancer-free. His story serves as another testament to the positive outcomes that can be achieved when one is committed to pursuing a good quality of life.

These two stories serve as powerful reminders that through commitment, we can achieve a high quality of life in all aspects. As I like to say, "Today's commitment is tomorrow's achievement!"

And that commitment is what's going to carry you forward as you learn about the nine key components of a quality life—joy, peace, patience, kindness, virtue, humility, temperance, faith, and love. We'll take each chapter and expound on them.

This book is my journey in search of a quality life. Many times, I felt stuck, frustrated with people and circumstances, and wondering how to make sense of this life that seemed unfair to me and my loved ones. In my quest, I came across these nine key components, and what I learned from them changed my perspective on life forever. Drawing from my personal encounters with these components, I have penned them in a vulnerable yet practical manner that aims to resonate with you and offer actionable insights for your own journey.

Are you stressed about your future, depressed about the past, or anxious when things are not as you expected? Are you waiting indefinitely, yearning for true love, feeling worthless, struggling with insecurities, or caught in the rat race of life—constantly searching but never finding what you truly yearn for? If any of these resonate with you, or if you feel like there is more to life than what you currently have—a deeper meaning, a greater purpose, a bigger reason that you yearn for but can't seem to find—then this book is for you.

I don't want you to just read about these nine components I'm about to share. At the end of each chapter, you'll have an opportunity to reflect on your own life and take practical steps in your journey to a quality life.

—◆—

Chapter One
JOY
Experiencing Lasting Joy

✦

The first time I went skiing was incredibly memorable and fascinating! After an hour of training, the instructor left, and my wife and I continued to practice on the bunny hill. As I practiced, I fell several times, either because kids skied across my path or because I hadn't yet learned how to snowplow to control my speed.

There were spots that I really didn't want to crash into and embarrass myself. But interestingly, the more I focused on avoiding those spots, the more I seemed to head in their direction and crash. Sometimes, I would intentionally fall on my back before reaching those spots, as it seemed less embarrassing.

It took me some time to learn how to prevent myself from crashing into those spots or even from falling. I needed to gain better control. Initially, I would go wherever the skis took me, but once I mastered control of them, I could guide them in the direction I desired.

This experience taught me a valuable object lesson about the joys of life. As we constantly focus on the negative and complain, we are steering ourselves towards a negative path.

The brain isn't inherently wired to seek out positives from birth. It develops based on the different experiences we encounter, especially during the formative years when exploration is key.

Think of it like the skis. If we don't train it in the direction we want it to go, it will lead us in unexpected ways, potentially causing us to crash in places we'd rather avoid. By training the brain to ski in the desired direction, we can guide it to follow the path we set. This doesn't guarantee a smooth journey without obstacles or distractions, like children skiing across our path or others crashing into us. However, we will possess the resilience to rise after a fall and persist on our skiing route.

Most of us, unfortunately, let our brain lead us in the direction it desires, and we often accept it as our inevitable fate. As a result, we fail to recognize the potential of a different or better outcome, rather than crashing in places we could have avoided. Here are some common ways we allow our brains to "crash" in negativity:

1. **Self-fulfilling prophecies**: These often originate from low self-esteem. Many constantly dwell on potential negative outcomes, inadvertently shaping them into their reality. In some cases, these outcomes become their inevitable destination. For instance, in relationships, if one is haunted by insecurities and fears that their partner might leave them because of their past mistakes or weaknesses, they might try to maintain control out of desperation. They may even resort to manipulation, desperately clinging to their partner at any cost. Unfortunately, this approach tends to backfire; despite their genuine desire to hold onto their partner, their actions inadvertently suffocate their partner. As a result, the partner might start to feel trapped and eventually choose to end the relationship, not out of a desire to cause pain, but because they felt stifled and manipulated.

2. **Pessimism:** This often originates from unresolved past experiences, cognitive biases, personality traits, and environmental factors (such as family dynamics, social influences, and cultural factors). It may contribute to a mindset characterized by negative expectations and a tendency to focus on potential pitfalls. For instance, one might have received an untraditional and uncommon incentive of $10,000 in their work, but they are not happy because there was a colleague who received $10,100. Of course, this is an exaggeration, but it can't be denied. Instead of focusing on the incredible incentive they received, the pessimist feels jealous and dissatisfied that another person has received $100 more. Can you relate with this person in other situations?

There may be other outcomes, but you get the point. So, how do we work on these types of issues and secure joy in our lives? As we saw earlier, if you keep looking at a spot you wish to avoid without mastering all the aspects of skiing, the ski will inevitably take you there and cause you to crash.

Similarly, without understanding the brain and how to redirect our thoughts, we too will crash into negativity. That's why we have to slow down and rewire our brains in a new direction.

Rewiring Your Brain for Optimism

I had to learn how to snowplow to gain control of my skis and be able to steer them. Likewise, we must learn to slow our negative thoughts so that we can steer our brains in a different direction. You determine the path you want your brain to ski. If you're seeking joy in life, then you must concentrate on joy. It's as simple as that.

What brings you joy? Learning to focus on the positive things more will be step one. Over time, as you direct your thoughts toward joy, your mind will more easily turn this way rather than toward negativity.

> *"Best skiers know how to fall."*

To be clear, though, by no means am I saying that it's going to be easy to shift toward looking at life positively, but it's definitely possible. As we intentionally focus on looking for positives in every situation, it will become a habit and our brain will be rewired to do just that. Similar to skiing, it will take a few falls to master it, but once we achieve mastery, it becomes much easier.

Again, this doesn't mean that people who have mastered the sport of skiing never fall. In fact, the place where my wife and I first skied had a cute little note that said, "Best skiers know how to fall." Falling can happen to the best of them, but they see it as a part of the process and not their fate. Likewise, when we do fall into a negative mindset, we can always get back up and work on that positive mindset.

As I gathered my thoughts to write this chapter, I remembered something basic but very essential for life right now. For those who have faith in Jesus, the hope of going to heaven and experiencing life on the new earth gives us purpose and meaning in this life. In heaven, we will joyfully recount the remarkable things God bestowed upon us during our time on this challenging earth. In that blissful realm, the memories of our hardships will fade away, and only the moments of God's grace and joy will remain vivid.

How do I know? *Revelation 21:4* conveys a powerful message: *"And God will wipe away every tear from their eyes; there shall be no more death, nor sorrow, nor crying. There shall be no more pain, for the former things have passed away."*

If this is the promise of heaven and the new earth, then why not begin preparing for it now? Why not focus on the positive aspects of life and let go of the negativity that weighs us down? As we embrace the hope of a future free from suffering and pain, why not strive to cultivate an empowering mindset that aligns with the purity and joy of heaven right here, right now?

The rest of this chapter will look at practical ways we can do just that.

Uplifting Music

Have you ever noticed that when you listen to music, your emotions react to the type of music you are listening to? Music has a significant impact on our brains and emotions, which is why it's often used in movies to evoke specific feelings during certain scenes. Whether people realize it or not, music plays a big part in our lives, for better or for worse. It has shaped and continues to shape our personalities and moods, impacting us both in the short term and the long term.

While music can be used for good or bad, why don't we use it for our good? Listening to uplifting music and encouraging words helps us to have a positive outlook on life. When we intentionally surround ourselves with music and messages that inspire and uplift us, we create an environment conducive to personal growth and well-being.

Yet, despite the undeniable benefits, many of us underestimate the potential of music as a tool for positivity. It could be due to a lack of awareness regarding its transformative power. Or we simply fall into the habit of consuming whatever music is readily available without considering its impact on our mood and mindset. Moreover, societal norms and cultural influences tend to prioritize music for entertainment over its potential for intentional personal growth.

However, by recognizing the profound influence of music on our emotions and consciously choosing to engage with uplifting content, we can harness its potential for our own benefit. Whether through curated playlists, motivational podcasts, or inspirational lyrics, we have the opportunity to cultivate a positive environment inside us which in turn helps us have a positive outlook on life.

I encourage you to incorporate this practice into your routine for a week and experience firsthand the transformative power it can have on your overall well-being. Give it a chance, and you'll see the difference it can make in your daily life.

Some of my go-to music for feeling calm, peaceful, and joyful come from the YouTube channel Give Glory 2 Him. If you are searching for uplifting music, check out this channel.

A Journey of True Achievements

The idea that success or achievement has to be immediate is a myth that diminishes the quality of joy in our lives. Many people find themselves striving to prove their worth to others, whether it be through showcasing their wealth, fame, intelligence, or religious beliefs. However, when this mindset dominates our thoughts, we often sacrifice our own happiness in the relentless pursuit of validation and approval from external sources in an attempt to reaffirm our self-worth.

When we remove this misconception from our minds, we can perform at our best without anticipating immediate results. It's common to think, I put in the effort, so I deserve recognition or success immediately, but life doesn't always operate on that timeline. Sometimes, you may have to endure times when results aren't visible despite your maximum effort, and that endurance builds resilience. You'll grow stronger and find satisfaction in knowing you gave it your all.

> "Whatever your hand finds to do, do it with your might; for there is no work or device or knowledge or wisdom in the grave where you are going" (Ecclesiastes 9:10).

> "A man will be satisfied with good by the fruit of his mouth, and the recompense of a man's hands will be rendered to him" (Proverbs 12:14).

> "And let us not grow weary while doing good, for in due season we shall reap if we do not lose heart" (Galatians 6:9).

These verses bring out two important points: First, always strive to do your best, and second, remember that your efforts will not go unrewarded. The teachings in the Bible consistently emphasize the idea that the fruits of our labor will eventually be recognized, even though the timing of these rewards may not be immediate.

However, who will appreciate your dedication? Recognition for hard work is essential because we as humans long to be recognized. Even so, while people's recognition can serve as a great motivator, the ultimate acknowledgment comes from God. For those who don't believe in God, and thus do not see immediate results from their efforts, finding joy in life can be challenging, potentially diminishing their quality of life. On the other hand, those who have faith in God can entrust the outcomes of their endeavors to Him, making them better suited for heaven.

Consider the heavenly angels and their tireless work. Sent by God, they diligently serve each and every person in the world—over eight billion. While not everyone will make it to heaven due to their own poor choices, the angels persist in their efforts, hoping for the best outcomes. Nevertheless, they entrust the final results to God's hands, thereby maintaining the joy that heaven brings.

The angels feel sadness when humans make wrong choices despite their unwavering dedication. However, their faith in God's ultimate plan sustains them, allowing them to continue their work with hope and perseverance.

Consider the scenario if the angels were to stop their work for us because they were tired of our poor choices. What if they were to quit because they weren't witnessing immediate results from their diligent efforts? Or, conversely, what if they based their joy solely on their hard work and anticipated immediate outcomes in the choices we make?

Fortunately, the angels remain steadfast in their service, trusting in God's ultimate plan and persevering despite the difficulties they may encounter. Their unwavering commitment serves as a testament to their faith in God and dedication to assisting us, even in the face of uncertainty and adversity.

Recently, I began creating thought-provoking spiritual videos to share on social media. I felt a sense of peace that God wanted me to proceed, and my wife was supportive of this journey. Initially, it went well, and I saw positive results. However, over time, the momentum slowed down, leading to frustration.

Two things exacerbated the situation. For one, I assumed that some would mock me for the low traction of my videos. And second, those who produced less meaningful videos were flourishing. This left me feeling dejected and sad.

I confided in my wife, expressing my frustration about working hard for God and expecting more significant results. I felt disappointed that God seemed inactive in helping me expand the reach of the videos He impressed me to share on social media. I kept complaining that evening that God was the one who gave me peace to start it, but He wasn't helping me.

My wife's response was wise, and it gave me perfect peace and joy. Since then, I haven't worried about whether others mock my videos with low views or whether people make silly videos and get more views. I saw this ministry from a totally different perspective.

"In heaven, we will see the fruits of your labor."

She reminded me, "Do you remember when Jesus hung on the cross? How many were there to support and encourage Him at that moment? He didn't see the results right away, not even from His disciples. Don't worry about seeing immediate results; instead, keep faithfully creating your videos. In heaven, we will see the fruits of your labor."

This made perfect sense! I thought about Noah who preached about the flood for at least a century, and no one got into the ark but his family. Moses didn't get to see the Israelites occupy the land of Canaan while he was alive. Stephen didn't see the conversion of Paul. There are many such examples in the Bible that confirm this reality.

> *"By placing all outcomes in God's hands, we become better prepared for heaven."*

The only reality we need to focus on is whether we are doing God's will. Don't work with the expectation of immediate results; instead, entrust your efforts to God's hands. Work only because it's what God calls you to do. When you labor according to God's will, don't fret over the outcomes; simply do your best, knowing that the results are ultimately in God's control, not yours.

This realization will lift a significant burden from your shoulders, allowing you to rediscover joy in your life. First Corinthians 3:6–9 illustrates the collaborative nature of our work with God. In this passage, Paul explains that while he planted and Apollos (a contemporary of Paul) watered, it was ultimately God who brought about the growth. Therefore, neither the one who plants nor the one who waters holds the ultimate result; rather, it is God who gives the increase according to His perfect time.

By placing all outcomes in God's hands, we become better

prepared for heaven. Again, what does heaven have to do with this? Heaven isn't designed to conform to our timeframes or our limited vision; rather, we must strive to align ourselves with the principles of heaven by surrendering our lives and the results of our efforts to a God that has higher thoughts than ours and can see the bigger picture:

> *"'For My thoughts are not your thoughts, nor are your ways My ways,' says the LORD. 'For as the heavens are higher than the earth, so are My ways higher than your ways, and My thoughts than your thoughts'"* (Isaiah 55:8–9).

Joy in Gratitude

Have you ever found yourself in a group setting where you're asked to share something you're thankful for about the people around you? Sometimes, I've been in such situations where I dislike a certain person, but I'm compelled to think of something positive to share about them. Despite my initial reluctance, I find that after some reflection, I can recall something good about them.

In those moments, when I express appreciation for someone I dislike, I feel a sense of joy bubbling in my heart. It's a profound realization that even those we may perceive negatively have positive attributes worth acknowledging.

If you haven't participated in such an activity, I highly recommend it. You'll likely discover that those you once considered entirely bad are not as bad as you imagined. Everyone possesses something good within them that we can appreciate. It just takes intentional effort from our end to recognize and remember it. Likewise, in every situation and experience in life, there exists some good that we can appreciate. No matter how dire a circumstance may appear, there's always a lesson to be learned and something positive to be gleaned from it. It merely requires intentional effort to rewire our brains to see the good in everyone and in every life situation.

I vividly recall when I first met my wife. We worked together in the same place, and her relentlessly positive attitude towards everything and everyone initially made me wonder. I found myself thinking, Okay, Pollyanna, who are you really? However, it didn't take long for me to realize that her positivity was genuine; it was simply her true personality shining through. Her presence felt like a breath of fresh air. She was consistently pleasant and a joy to work with. In contrast, I felt ashamed of my own judgmental and complaining nature.

As my wife and I were courting and getting to know each other, she shared with me a transformative story that had profoundly impacted her. In 2013, she came across the story of Ann Voskamp, the author of the book One Thousand Gifts. Ann's life was marked by tragedy from a young age when her baby sister was killed in a tragic accident, leading to her mother's institutionalization due to trauma and her father's descent into depression. As a teenager, Ann saw only pain and suffering in life, which convinced her that God brought only hardship. As a result, she struggled with depression and suicidal thoughts.

As an adult, and a mother and wife, Ann still struggled with those thoughts. Her perspective shifted, though, when a friend challenged her to document 1,000 gifts of thanksgiving. Though initially skeptical, Ann accepted the challenge, and her life was forever changed. Through this practice, she began to recognize the myriad blessings God bestowed upon her every day, from simple joys like the air flowing through her hair and the jelly on top of her toast to a colorful sunset. This shift in mindset transformed her outlook on life, leading her to challenge others to embark on the same journey of gratitude by writing three things daily that they are grateful for.

Inspired by Ann's story, my wife took up the challenge, incorporating it into her evening bedtime routine. Despite the stresses of each day, she would count the blessings. She says doing so felt like a "sleeping pill" that helped her relax and find peace. Through this practice, she learned that in every circumstance there is something she can be grateful for. This changed my wife's outlook on life to be more positive.

As Ann herself says, "Busy is a choice, stress is a choice, giving yourself to joy is a choice, choose well."[1]

I was truly amazed by my wife's experience. By looking at a real-life example, I learned the profound impact gratitude has on fostering constant joy. I must admit, I'm still in the learning phase of cultivating gratitude in every situation. However, I can confidently say that as I grow in this practice, I feel a profound sense of joy blossoming in my life. It's a type of joy that I've been unable to find elsewhere.

Gratitude is strongly associated with an individual's well-being, according to numerous studies.

Psychologists Dr. Robert A. Emmons and Dr. Michael E.

McCullough conducted research on gratitude, asking participants to write a few sentences each week about particular topics.[2]

The participants were divided into three groups:
- Group 1 focused on things they were grateful for.
- Group 2 wrote about daily irritations or things that displeased them.
- Group 3 wrote about events that had affected them, without an emphasis on positivity or negativity.

After ten weeks, those who wrote about gratitude reported the following[3]:
- Increased optimism and life satisfaction
- Higher levels of physical activity and fewer visits to physicians

Another researcher, Dr. Martin E.P. Seligman of the University of Pennsylvania, tested positive psychology interventions on 411 people. In this study, participants who wrote and delivered a letter of gratitude experienced a significant increase in happiness scores. This intervention had a greater impact than any other intervention and led to benefits lasting for a month.[4]

Other research has found that expressing gratitude in relationships[5]:
- Increases positive feelings toward a partner.
- Encourages open communication about relationship concerns.

And finally, in the workplace, managers who express gratitude may motivate employees to work harder. A study at the Wharton School at the University of Pennsylvania found that fundraisers who received a message of gratitude made 50% more calls than those who did not.[6]

These research studies show that maintaining gratitude despite life's challenges can positively impact various aspects of well-being, ultimately leading people to a joy-filled, quality life. Joy isn't merely a reaction to external influences; rather, it's a conscious state of mind that persists through different situations, fueled by gratitude. Yes, gratitude is undeniably one of the most powerful means for joy. While it may be challenging to accept and fully embrace it, the truth remains unchanged. This psychological principle requires deliberate daily practice to help joy become an integral part of your life.

> *"Joy isn't merely a reaction to external influences; rather, it's a conscious state of mind that persists through different situations, fueled by gratitude."*

While everyone desires joy in life, achieving it requires conscious effort and cognitive reasoning. Just like other emotions, joy can be orchestrated by our thoughts and perceptions. For example, one person may find themselves surrounded by friends, yet feel sad and depressed, while another may feel perfectly content and joyful while alone in their room, writing a book about improving quality of life.

Sadly, many individuals choose to dwell on the pessimistic aspects of life, enveloped in gloom and negativity.

Throughout history, we have witnessed numerous examples of individuals who, in their most challenging moments, chose to adopt a different attitude towards life than the majority of us do. These examples stand as some of the greatest testaments in world history.

Take, for instance, the experience of Paul and Silas in Acts 16:20–24. They were unfairly beaten when Paul cast out a demon in Jesus' name. They were conspired against, mistreated, and put in an inner prison with their feet in stocks. Typically, individuals in such distress and discomfort due to their confinement would moan, complain, and curse, but Paul and Silas surprised the others by singing praises and praying instead. They found joy in suffering for Christ's sake. This experience likely helped Paul empathize with the suffering he once caused others before his conversion.

Suddenly, an earthquake shook the prison, opening all the doors and loosening everyone's chains. The jailer, fearing that the prisoners had escaped and he would be punished, prepared to kill himself. However, Paul stopped him, assuring him that all the prisoners were still there. This act of integrity and compassion led the jailer to inquire about salvation, and Paul and Silas shared the gospel with him and his household, resulting in their conversion.

This event shows the evidence of Paul and Silas's gratitude to God. They took it as their privilege to suffer for Christ and trust in His ultimate plan and guidance. Despite their own suffering, Paul and Silas seized the opportunity to share the message of salvation with the jailer and his household. Their actions demonstrated a desire to bring others into a relationship with God and reflected a deep gratitude for the transformative power of the gospel in their own lives.

After several personal experiences, Paul said, *"Rejoice always, pray without ceasing, in everything give thanks; for this is the will of God in Christ Jesus for you" (1 Thessalonians 5:16–18).*

In conclusion, I invite you to consider the potential outcomes of embracing the principles discussed in this chapter, even if you disagree with me about the existence of God. By sincerely practicing optimism, listening to uplifting music, not waiting for immediate results, and having gratitude, you have the opportunity to live a joyful and fulfilling life, regardless of your beliefs. In doing so, you not only enhance your own well-being but also become a beacon of inspiration for others.

If this is the only time we'll ever have to live, isn't it worth striving for a quality life? Think about it!

Reflections:
1. Have you experienced self-fulfilling prophecies in your life? What were they?
2. What are three steps you can take now to rewire your brain to focus on the positive aspects of life? (Example: Challenge negative thoughts and replace them with more positive and empowering ones.)
3. Write five things you do that give you real joy in life. (Example: Engaging in creative activities like painting, writing, or playing music)
4. What are ten successes or achievements in your life that were not immediate? Write them down so you can go through them when you need some encouragement.
5. List different negative things that have happened in your life. Write down what positive things or life lessons resulted from those negative experiences. Write down at least two a week until you exhaust the list.
6. Write two to five things you are thankful for every day.

References:
1. Ann Voskamp, *The Broken Way* (Zondervan, 2016), 128.
2. "Giving Thanks Can Make You Happier," Harvard Health Publishing, Aug. 14, 2021, www.health.harvard.edu/healthbeat/giving-thanks-can-make-you-happier.
3. Ibid.
4. Ibid.
5. Ibid.
6. Ibid.

Chapter Two

PEACE

Are You A Hoarder?

I visited a church member, Bill, at his apartment for the first time, and I was shocked upon entering. It took a few seconds to realize the mess I had stepped into. The apartment was filled with books, mail, clothes, costumes (he was a local stage actor), props, and several other things littered around. Yes, Bill was a hoarder! The apartment smelled like cat litter and cigar smoke combined. Because of that, it was hard for me to breathe freely. I would take a deep breath while covering my nose and then slowly exhale. Of course, he didn't know I was struggling with the smell because I didn't want him to be embarrassed.

I also didn't want to touch anything in that apartment because most of the things were covered with dust and cat hair. But there were two couches draped with sheets, and that's where Bill and I would sit and chat for some time. I felt bad for him, so I volunteered to dedicate two hours every Sunday until the apartment was cleaned. Bill had a big smile on his face that said, "Thank you."

The next Sunday I started cleaning the dirty dishes that filled the sink and overflowed to the drying rack and even to the floor next to the sink. It took almost an hour, but I was proud of myself when that task was accomplished.

After the dishes I decided to clean the pantry. I sorted the canned food and had to throw away most of it because the cans were expired. Some had been expired for more than ten years. While I was sorting, though, Bill wanted to go through everything before I threw it away because he wanted to keep some of the canned foods even if they were expired for over a year. I laughed to myself at his concern.

By the time I sorted the food, my two hours had passed. I happily drove home knowing that I had done a good deed that day. I returned to his apartment the following Sunday and was shocked to find the sink again filled with dirty dishes. Though this Sunday was not as bad as the previous one, it still upset me to know that Bill didn't take the responsibility of doing his own dishes during the week. I started to wonder whether I actually was doing a good deed by helping Bill clean. Was I just making a perfectly capable man disabled? So, I didn't do his dishes this time but continued with other areas of the apartment.

I came across a whole lot of things that I was very sure he wasn't using on a regular basis. However, he insisted that he keep all of them. So, I just cleaned and organized them. Thankfully, he did throw away a whole bunch of mail, keeping only a few necessary pieces. A couple weeks passed by, and there was still a lot to clean, so I decided to ask for some help from my church.

A couple from church, who are also very good friends of mine, agreed to help me clean his place. We went as a team and cleaned the whole apartment as much as possible. We opened the windows wide so that fresh air could circulate and sunlight could come in and brighten the apartment. We scrubbed the floors and walls so well that there were no more marks or stains.

Finally, I sighed with relief, knowing that the apartment looked much better, smelled pretty good, and didn't have any more cat hair or litter on the floor. Now, Bill could enjoy a better place to live.

But unfortunately, I returned to visit him after a couple months, and it broke my heart to see that the place was back to how it looked on my first visit.

Now, it's easy for us to think, If he had kept up with cleaning his apartment, it wouldn't have gone back to that messy condition. And it's true that he should've gotten rid of all the unnecessary things and kept his apartment clean with just the necessary things. But was keeping unnecessary things the root problem? Or was there something else that needed to be fixed so that he wouldn't hoard?

Here are some things I noticed about Bill's problem:

1. Not a one-day event: Bill didn't accumulate all the things he "needed" and become a hoarder in just one day. It was a continual gathering of various items over time.
2. Intentional saving: Bill might have stored food in anticipation of future shortages, saved his diverse props and costumes for potential stage performances, or set aside mail to sort through later. In his mind, there was always a "purpose" behind saving things. However, items began to pile up overwhelmingly, making it difficult for him to let go.
3. Holding onto useless things: Before I discarded some items, Bill would always inspect them, deciding what to keep and what to toss. He always insisted on keeping a few items he didn't need, such as old promotional mail,

expired food cans, and in some cases, things he couldn't even identify.
4. Comfortable in the chaos: Bill might have recognized the need to clean and organize his living space, but he hadn't taken any action for years. Upon entering the apartment for the first time, I noticed that he had created narrow pathways between all his things to access different areas of his home. He was content in his apartment as long as he had enough space to walk.
5. Playing the victim: During my initial visit to Bill's house, he explained why his home looked the way it did. He mentioned undergoing leg surgery following an accident, which caused him severe pain and made it difficult to move. Consequently, he struggled to navigate to the kitchen or bathroom. However, as Bill and I spent more time together, I realized that his level of handicap wasn't as severe as he portrayed it to be. Despite claiming difficulty with mobility, he managed to go up and down a flight of stairs, drive to nearby places, walk from the parking lot to buildings, and engage in various activities. He wasn't faking his handicap for others to believe but rather internalizing it and restricting himself from activities he was fully capable of.
6. Preferring the mess: Bill neglected regular cleaning and organization of his home so that it soon became cluttered with books, mail, clothes, and various items once again. Why did he neglect cleaning his living space? It almost seemed as though he preferred a cluttered environment.

Now that we've considered Bill's problem of hoarding, take a moment to reflect deeply within yourself. Search your heart and see whether you resonate with the traits of a hoarder. Do you find joy in accumulating possessions over many years, storing them away just in case you need them, even if they serve no practical purpose? Have you grown accustomed to living amid clutter, finding comfort in its presence? Do you sometimes believe you have limitations or handicaps that cannot be changed?

Pause for a moment, meditate on these questions, and answer them honestly. If you find that you don't align with any of these characteristics, then congratulations!

So, why are we contemplating the story of a hoarder in a chapter about peace? There's a crucial connection between the two. Hoarding is actually a mental health condition that involves persistent difficulty in parting with possessions. It involves accumulating multiple items that are unnecessary, resulting in severe clutter.

But there is also another kind of clutter.

Consider these questions: Are you holding a grudge against someone who bullied or cheated you? Have you bottled up resentment against someone? Have you experienced abuse and struggled to forgive the abuser? Do you feel consistently rejected by loved ones due to past trauma? Are you unable to forgive your parent(s) for their absence during your upbringing? Do you struggle to let go of work stress even in a non-work environment?

If you answered yes to at least one of these questions, you are a hoarder, too. I call this type of hoarding "emotional hoarding." While it might not look like Bill's physical clutter, accumulating stress from trauma, work, relationships, and poverty manifests as low self-esteem, fear of the future, irritability, a short temper, an unkind personality, and controlling or avoidant behaviors. Though stress is unfortunately a part of life, it can unknowingly pile up and cause harm to you and those around you when left unaddressed.

In Bill's case study, we identified six factors that contributed to his hoarding behavior. Now, let's explore the possible similarities between his physical hoarding and emotional hoarding:

1. Not a one-day event: Did the negative emotions accumulate gradually over time, rather than all at once?
2. Intentional saving: Have you been deliberately holding onto past wrongs, replaying them frequently to keep them fresh in your mind?
3. Holding onto useless things: Do you keep reminders of past events out of necessity, or have those reminders become so a part of your identity that you fear losing yourself if you let go?
4. Comfortable in the chaos: Do you find comfort in tumultuous relationships, so much so that normalcy is strange? Are you comfortable manipulating others to get what you want in relationships?
5. Playing the victim: Do you seek constant care and attention by portraying yourself as a victim of past mistreatment?
6. Preferring the mess: Do you avoid addressing emotional baggage and instead find comfort in negativity, pushing people away to shield yourself from hurt? Do you hurt others in anticipation of being hurt yourself?

Letting Go of Emotional Hoarding

I've encountered several women at different stages of my life who struggled to see men in a positive light, favoring women in most situations. It was an intriguing observation for me. Whenever there was a conflict between a man and a woman, whether in a romantic relationship or a friendship, these women tended to blame the man and support the woman, even when it was evident that the woman was at fault.

These women found it difficult to acknowledge women's mistakes and were more inclined to be forgiving towards them rather than towards men. I pondered on the reason behind this tendency.

Upon closer observation, I noticed a similar pattern among them. They all shared a history of bitter experiences with their ex-husbands. They had all been mistreated by these men, leading them to harbor animosity towards all men unbeknownst to them.

Due to these painful encounters, they held onto resentment towards their ex-husbands who had treated them poorly. Unfortunately, this bitterness shaped their view of all men, causing them to approach them with suspicion and a lack of kindness.

However, there is some good news here. When some of these women recognized the turmoil they had been going through for years because of their past, they decided that they didn't want to live that way anymore. They didn't want to hoard unnecessary ill feelings towards their ex-husbands because doing so was taking a toll on their health.

Subsequently, they sought forgiveness from God for holding onto resentment towards their ex-husbands. They also forgave their ex-husbands wholeheartedly. This doesn't mean they went back to their abusive husbands or unhealthy situations, but they forgave and decluttered their minds of the resentment in order to move on with their lives. This act brought them freedom and peace. Today, some of these women who forgave their husbands are transformed and liberated individuals.

Unforgiveness isn't exclusive to women because men go through these issues as well. We all at some point face challenges, such as being treated unfairly, bullied, cheated on, or manipulated, whether it be in relationships, school, or the workplace.

Unfortunately, many haven't experienced the freedom and peace that comes through forgiveness. I can't even imagine the countless individuals around the world who have had bitter experiences in their lives and continue to hoard resentment, vengeance, low self-esteem, and more. This emotional hoarding not only weighs heavily on them but also has a ripple effect, impacting those in their lives.

So, how do we let go of emotional hoarding? First and foremost, fixing any type of issue requires recognizing that there is an issue. By acknowledging the issue, you are already on the path to improvement. If you don't believe there is an issue, then you won't see a need to change. Introspection is always your best friend. Be brutally honest with yourself and analyze the situation. This can also be helpful for different types of mental health issues, though I encourage you to do so with the help of a mental health professional.

Many times, we are unaware of our problems, but by claiming the following verse, you are asking God to clearly reveal the areas in your life that need attention:

> "Search me, O God, and know my heart; try me, and know my anxieties; and see if there is any wicked way in me, and lead me in the way everlasting" (Psalm 139:23-24).

If you find yourself unable to process the situation or feel the need for an impartial evaluation, I suggest you seek out a mental health professional who can guide you in the process of dealing with resentment and unhealthy patterns.

You will also find an activity at the end of this chapter. Take the time to answer all the questions thoroughly. Afterwards, share your responses with someone you love and trust—someone who won't use your answers against you but will instead offer their honest understanding to support you.

The activity can help you gain clarity and perspective on the situation at hand. By sharing your thoughts with a trusted loved one, you can benefit from their insights and support. Remember, the goal is not to seek validation but understanding and guidance. Your trusted confidant can offer a fresh outlook and help you see things from a different angle.

If you find yourself a emotional hoarder after going through the activity, there are two crucial steps to take: (1) recognizing the power of forgiveness and (2) recognizing the power of God. These two factors are interconnected and essential in achieving freedom and living a peaceful life.

Acknowledging and addressing our emotions and inner turmoil is crucial to improve our well-being and relationships. Hoarding grudges and resentment can weigh heavily on our hearts and minds, affecting our mental and emotional health. They will also eventually affect our physical health.

Learning to forgive, both ourselves and others, is a powerful step towards healing and moving forward in a positive direction. Forgiveness, when wholehearted, gives you freedom and peace in your life. By letting go of past hurt and embracing forgiveness, we open the door to healing and personal growth. Remember, forgiveness is a gift we give ourselves.

But how do you forgive someone who has treated you unfairly? This is where the power of God comes into play. By ourselves, it's not easy to forgive, but with God's strength, it becomes possible. As you surrender to God all your grudges, resentment, or whatever negative emotions you have hoarded, you will find a sense of relief and liberation.

Recognizing the power of God won't help you forgive unless you make an intentional effort towards it. Likewise, recognizing the power of forgiveness won't help you unless you receive strength from God to forgive. They go hand in hand.

Of course, the feelings won't leave you magically. After all, you might have harbored the emotions for months, years, or even decades. The longer you have hoarded these emotions, the stronger the neural pathways have become. It requires intentional effort on your part to stop entertaining grudges or resentment, and with God's help, you will find the strength to say no each time a negative thought arises in your mind.

As you continue to say no consistently, the negative thoughts will grow weaker and weaker, and you will feel the burden lifted from you. Freedom will begin to set in. You will notice that you're not as irritated as you were before. You will stop hurting the people in your life.

If you come across another abusive situation, you will recognize it sooner and step out of that relationship quicker. When you reflect on your past, you will see it as a victor, not as a victim. Own the victory!

Cleaning Out Unwanted Things in Life

Imagine if your neighbor dumps trash in your yard a few times, causing it to spread all over. Naturally, you would be upset by their actions. Let's say, instead of talking to your neighbor and fixing the situation by the necessary means, you gather up the trash and bring it inside your house, intending to keep it as evidence for potential future consequences. However, as time passes, you refuse to dispose of it, even though the garbage truck comes weekly for pickup.

The trash begins to decay, emitting a foul odor and attracting flies and worms. Despite these issues, you hold onto it, eagerly awaiting the *"judgment day."* Unfortunately, your decision to hoard the trash not only affects your health but also impacts your loved ones at home and visitors alike. Meanwhile, the neighbor may have continued disposing of their trash responsibly or even shifted their dumping to other yards in the neighborhood.

You continue to hold onto the hope that one day, the neighbor will face the consequences of their actions. Let's say that the judgment day comes, and they are caught and penalized. Will it undo the harm that weeks, months, or years of living with the decaying trash has caused you and your loved ones? What if the neighbor acknowledges their wrongdoing and begins properly disposing of their trash?

Just like hoarding trash in your house, holding onto resentment can negatively impact your mental and emotional well-being, as well as affect those around you. Even if the person responsible is eventually held accountable or makes amends, the damage caused by hoarding negative emotions may not easily be undone. It's essential to address conflicts and grievances directly, communicate effectively, and seek resolution by forgiving the person for the sake of your own well-being and the health of your other relationships.

I understand how it feels to question why misfortune seems to happen to us instead of to those who caused harm. It's natural to wonder why our health may suffer while the wrongdoers thrive without consequences, seemingly happy and unaffected. Remember, judgment will eventually come, and everyone will answer for their actions. Let's focus on not letting unforgiveness burden us.

When we fixate on the wrongs done to us, we allow the wrongdoer to reside in our minds rent-free. They occupy our thoughts, replaying the hurtful incidents over and over. Have you heard of the phrase *"repetition deepens impression"*? It fits perfectly in this situation. Repetition solidifies memories, reinforcing the negative impact.

Clearing out those negative emotions from our lives, including thoughts of the person and the misfortune they brought—just like we remove trash from our house and yard—allows us to have a healthier environment to live in. Find peace in knowing that God will eventually right all wrongs.

Negative Outcome of Unforgiveness

Unfortunately, not everyone chooses to give up on their vengeance or resentment. Some hold on to it as their identity. They may use that unfortunate experience from their past as an excuse for all the mistakes they make in their lives. Although the experience might have been a significant misfortune, they choose to dwell on it as if it were their fate.

I've been acquainted with some people who have hoarded resentment for over half a century. Either they see it as too much to process and work on, or they outright don't want to forget what was done to them and prefer to hold a grudge. If only they knew the impact it has on them and those around them!

Some individuals take pride in their suffering, seeing it as unique to them and integral to their identity. They fear that letting go of this suffering would mean losing a part of themselves. To justify it, they say, "You haven't gone through this, so you don't understand me." However, this should not be an excuse for being unforgiving.

This unforgiving mindset not only prevents a liberated and peaceful life but also causes major health issues. It can lead to diabetes, heart conditions, high cortisol levels, and even cancer. I used to work with cancer patients, and the majority of them held resentment toward a spouse, childhood abuser, or some other person who had hurt them. They found it hard to let go and thus had been hoarding the negative emotions for several years.

If you do some research on the topic of forgiveness, you'll find numerous articles, research papers, and books that delve into this topic, exploring the psychological, emotional, and physiological effects of forgiveness and unforgiveness. There is extensive research on forgiveness and its health benefits, as well as on unforgiveness and the health conditions that result.

The Story of the Staines Family

The Staines family incident, also known as the Graham Staines murder case, is a tragic event that occurred in Orissa, India, in January 1999. Graham Staines, an Australian Christian missionary working with leprosy patients, along with his two sons Philip (age 10) and Timothy (age 6), were brutally murdered by a group of radicals while they slept in their station wagon in the village of Manoharpur.

I still remember how my mum was saddened reading this in the newspaper. When she shared it with our family, I was young and didn't think much of it, but I knew it was really a bad incident. Growing up, I never forgot it, especially the response of Graham's wife, Gladys Staines, to the tragedy.

The attack sparked outrage and condemnation worldwide. Mrs. Staines, who also served in the mission alongside her husband but was not present during the attack, responded to this horrific act with remarkable grace and forgiveness.

Despite the immense pain and loss she experienced, Mrs. Staines chose to forgive those responsible for the murder of her husband and sons. In a profound act of forgiveness, she embodied the teachings of love and compassion that were central to her Christian faith.

> *"Mrs. Staines's ability to forgive in the face of such devastating loss stands as a testament to the power of God that will be given if we're willing."*

In the aftermath of the tragedy, Mrs. Staines, along with her daughter, continued her work among the leprosy patients in India, demonstrating resilience and a steadfast commitment to the mission she and her husband had dedicated their lives to.

Her forgiveness in the darkest of times became a powerful testimony of love and grace, inspiring many around the world, including myself. Mrs. Staines's ability to forgive in the face of such devastating loss stands as a testament to the power of God that will be given if we're willing.

Jesus on the Cross

Jesus, throughout His ministry, taught us powerful lessons essential for a quality life. One of the lessons He emphasized was forgiveness. He had to reiterate this teaching multiple times as it proved difficult for people to grasp. Here are a couple of examples that illustrate this point:

In *Luke 17:4*, Jesus states, *"And if he sins against you seven times in a day, and seven times in a day returns to you, saying, 'I repent,' you shall forgive him."*

In another instance, found in *Matthew 18:21–22*, Peter asked Jesus, *"Lord, how often shall my brother sin against me, and I forgive him? Up to seven times?"* Jesus responded, *"I do not say to you, up to seven times, but up to seventy times seven."*

Jesus reinforced the importance of forgiveness by sharing the parable of the unforgiving servant right after the above conversation. Part of truly receiving forgiveness from God involves extending that forgiveness to those who have wronged us. Do you remember the Lord's Prayer? Yes, Jesus mentions forgiveness there as well:

> *"And forgive us our debts, as we forgive our debtors. ... For if you forgive men their trespasses, your heavenly Father will also forgive you. But if you do not forgive men their trespasses, neither will your Father forgive your trespasses" (Matthew 6:12, 14–15).*

Since Jesus taught forgiveness so many times, did He follow what He preached? Let's take a look at *Luke 23:33–34*, a passage from the Crucifixion:

> *"And when they had come to the place called Calvary, there they crucified Him, and the criminals, one on the right hand and the other on the left. Then Jesus said, 'Father, forgive them, for they do not know what they do.' And they divided His garments and cast lots."*

This passage is powerful evidence that shows one can forgive in any circumstance. Even while Jesus was suffering pain from all the whiplashes, the thorny crown, and the nails pierced into His palms and feet, He was able to forgive those who tortured Him.

With all His agony and pain, He forgave them on the spot. If He could forgive in such extreme circumstances, we too can forgive those who wrong us.

Jesus' act of forgiveness on the cross serves as a profound example for all of us. Despite enduring unimaginable pain and suffering, He chose to forgive those who caused Him harm. This act of unconditional forgiveness showcases the depth of His love and mercy towards humanity. It reminds us that forgiveness is not only essential for our physical and emotional well-being but also for our spiritual growth.

By choosing forgiveness, we free ourselves from the burden of resentment and open our hearts to healing and peace. Let us draw inspiration from Jesus' remarkable display of forgiveness and strive to embody this virtue in our own lives, no matter how challenging it may seem.

The moment you forgive as Jesus did, God will give you the strength to have victory over the situation. Forgiveness is not a sign of weakness but a demonstration of strength. This strength will help you lead a peaceful life, which adds to the quality of life we all desire.

Reflections:
1. Write down the negative emotions you have towards someone or even yourself.
2. Write down approximately how long you have been hoarding this/these emotion(s).
3. Next write down the incident(s) that started all this turmoil in your mind.
4. How do these incident(s) threaten your present or

future self?
5. Can you do anything about it? If so, what? If it's something to do with others that you can't control, then what is something you can do?
6. Memorize three uplifting verses to recite every time you remember the negative incidents or develop negative emotions.

—◆—

Chapter Three
PATIENCE
Finding Purpose In Waiting

⋅ ✦ ⋅

Red Light

Imagine you're traveling and you come across a sequence of traffic lights, all of which turn red just as you approach. Each wait at a stoplight, even if it's only for 45 seconds to a minute, can feel like an eternity, especially when you encounter another red light less than a mile down the road. Many people find it hard to wait at traffic lights, even if they aren't pressed for time. It's because we have grown increasingly impatient in all aspects of life. Very few people enjoy the ride.

But there are a few lessons we can learn from the stoplight experience:
1. The red light is a protection.
2. Others are waiting, just like you are.
3. Once you start your journey, there's no turning back.
4. The red light is not your destination; it's just a pause.

Now, let's compare these with our lives:
1. **The red light is a protection**: Often, at a stoplight, we may not see the dangers ahead while we wait. The red light serves to protect us from accidents that could occur if someone were to run through it, risking not only their own safety but also that of others. In this way, a red light acts not as an inconvenience but as a safeguard.

Similarly, periods of waiting in our lives are not merely delays but valuable lessons in patience. We may not always grasp the bigger picture during these times, making the wait seem intolerable and our desire to rush forward overwhelming.

However, waiting patiently can significantly enhance our character. It provides us with an opportunity to reflect on our lives and gain clarity about our goals and destinations. This period of waiting allows us to better prepare for what's ahead, ensuring that when the time comes to move forward, we do so with greater wisdom and preparedness.

In late 2011, I made a pivotal decision to leave my job and pursue training in medical missionary work in Kenya. My last day of employment was the memorable date of 11.11.11. However, after resigning, I received no immediate communication from the missionary school, which sowed seeds of doubt and concern about the choice I had made. People around me questioned my decision. Some labeled me as lazy, and others said I was foolish for not staying at my job while I waited for the school to respond. Their reminders that I could have continued earning money during the wait only deepened my disappointment in myself.

By the beginning of December, with anxiety mounting, I reached out again to the school through email. This time, their prompt reply cleared the path for my journey, offering a profound sense of relief. Despite the affirmation of my forthcoming departure, the criticisms and questions from others during my period of waiting lingered in my mind.

Yet, it was in Kenya, amid my training, that I had my conversion experience and committed my life to Jesus Christ. This journey brought me closer to God than I had ever been, turning what I initially perceived as idleness into a significant period of spiritual growth. God revealed to me that the 48 days spent at home, previously seen as wasted time, were a necessary pause for deepening my spiritual connection with Him.

Up until those days, I had never prayed, except for three times a day before eating my meals. But during this time of *"idleness,"* I started reading my Bible and other spiritually encouraging books, and I prayed both in the morning and evening. These practices weren't just a filling of time; they were a deepening of my spiritual roots, preparing the soil of my soul for what was to come. This dedicated period of reflection and connection marked the beginning of a profound spiritual journey, culminating in a transformative conversion experience in Kenya.

This newfound spiritual foundation was crucial for my experience in Kenya, where I embraced missionary work with dedication. Without this period of spiritual preparation, I might have abandoned my mission prematurely and returned to India. My stay in the Simba hills, a place detached from the conveniences of electricity and reliable internet, underscored the reason behind the delayed communication from the missionary school and, more profoundly, facilitated my spiritual awakening.

This stoplight experience beautifully illustrates how periods of waiting or seeming inactivity can serve as crucial intervals for spiritual deepening and preparation for the experiences that await us. This chapter of my life taught me that life's priorities extend far beyond the pursuit of financial gain. It illustrated the importance of the patience and faith that guide us towards fulfilling our true calling from God.

2. **Others are waiting, just like you are**: It's easy to feel isolated in our waiting, as if we're the only ones paused at a crossroads, watching others move seamlessly towards their goals, be it financial success, health transformation, or career achievements. This perception can mislead us into believing that progress is a constant for others and obscure the reality that they, too, have had their moments of halt, whether before ours or sometime in the future. Not everyone has the stoplight experience at the same time.

Consider a four-way intersection: only one or two directions can proceed at a time while the others wait their turn. In life, the progress of others doesn't diminish our own prospects. It's a reminder to avoid comparisons. I've shared my frustrations of waiting with my wife on many occasions, but her wisdom always guides me back to a broader understanding. Through her lens, I'm reminded that we each travel a path marked by its unique challenges and timing.

Recently, I faced a seven-month delay in receiving my work permit to start working in the US. During this period, I couldn't shake the feeling that my life was at a standstill, especially when I saw everyone around me making strides in their careers or furthering their education. It seemed like everyone was accomplishing something meaningful in their lives, except for me.

However, my wife offered a perspective that shifted my entire outlook. She pointed out that this waiting period allowed me the unique opportunity to dedicate my time to writing this book you're currently reading. She reminded me that juggling a full-time job alongside writing would have significantly prolonged the process, likely extending it to at least 18 months to achieve what I have now.

Understanding this, I've learned to shift my focus from comparison to gratitude, recognizing the blessings God has granted me without measuring them against others' journeys. Everyone has a different journey, different roadblocks, different reroutes, and different destinations, and comparing them with yours is not a fair comparison. Remembering that we all at some point wait at stoplights and anticipate the moment we can advance encourages patience and fosters a sense of a communal journey, even in our distinct paths.

Another aspect to consider is the impatience we have while waiting to meet our significant others. Most of us know this struggle, don't we? How many single young people in their late twenties feel a sense of desperation and anxiety or feel like they are missing out on life? It becomes harder when we see all our friends, neighbors, colleagues, and relatives getting married and settling down while we are still searching for that special someone. It can truly feel like everyone else has been given the green light except for us.

The key here is to cultivate faith and patience for the timing God has planned for you. By exercising patience and trusting in His timing, you are more likely to find a partner who is truly compatible with you. Rushing ahead with your plans, driven by impatience or societal pressure, might only lead to detours and further delays in finding the right partner. Instead, consider the value of waiting for the match God has in store for you. Isn't someone worth waiting for also worth the patience this journey requires?

Imagine you're on your way to work. Your shift starts at 8:30 am, and you are just five minutes from the office, set to arrive at 8:28 am. Desperation kicks in when the traffic light turns red right before you can pass, and the traffic on all sides looks heavy. Worried you'll reach your job after 8:30 am and incur a fine, you contemplate running the red light in the final moments before you bring your car to a complete stop. Deciding to push through, you manage to reach the office parking lot by 8:27 am, but a police car pulls up behind you, lights flashing.

You clearly know why the cop pulled up behind you. Guess what, that day you didn't make it to your job on time. Ironically, despite your efforts to save time, you ended up late for work because you chose to bypass the waiting period. This scenario mirrors the journey of finding love. In haste, you might bypass the waiting period, fearing you're falling behind as others find their partners, but such impatience can lead you to miss out on meeting the love of your life. Therefore, it's crucial to wait a bit longer, allowing God to bring the right person into your life at the perfect time.

This doesn't mean waiting for the love of your life should be a passive endeavor. Venturing out to meet people, cultivating genuine friendships, sharing your journey, addressing insecurities, improving yourself, and forging connections with others are all part of being on the path toward your destination. Waiting is not about staying idle; it's an active period of self-improvement and growth with God's guidance.

Don't settle for just anyone out of convenience, but rather let God guide you. Once He signals the green light, you'll meet the love of your life. Are you willing to confidently trust God with your love life? Can you find peace in waiting for His green light, instead of succumbing to anxiety and desperation? *"He has made everything beautiful in its time" (Ecclesiastes 3:11).*

3. Once you start this journey, there's no turning back: Growth in life comes from continually moving forward. Consider the birth of a child: once born, a child cannot return to the mother's womb but must move forward and grow. The struggles and pain endured are for their development, and as they grow, they have the power to choose their experiences for good or for bad. Likewise, the process of enduring and growing to be a better person, without giving up, is a testament to one's patience.

A friend who works at a hospital recently shared with me about an extraordinary incident that happened during a childbirth: a baby's head emerged from the womb but then retracted back into the womb. This rare occurrence necessitated urgent surgical intervention since the baby, now able to breathe through its nose, couldn't survive long inside the mother. The doctors successfully performed surgery to deliver the baby safely. This type of delivery highlights a critical point: even newborns can't return to the womb. Once out, they must continue forward to grow.

Similarly, in life, while at a red light—a pause—it's tempting to want to retreat to a familiar or comfortable past even if it was a horrible experience. However, these moments of pause are temporary and not our final destination. They are designed for us to grow in patience and prepare for what's ahead. We must resist the urge to retreat like the newborn and instead focus on moving forward, embracing growth and the journey that lies ahead.

Fortunately, you do have a rearview mirror through which you can reflect on your life's journey, learning from both the good and bad experiences. This reflection enables you to use those lessons for a better future and to become a better person, but it requires dedication and patience. Are you willing to wait patiently for your turn to move forward?

Consider the Israelites: Under God's guidance, Moses led them out of Egypt towards the land of Canaan, promising freedom. However, at every trial, their immediate reaction was to consider reversing course and continuing in their servitude. Despite the harshness of slavery, it was a familiar discomfort, and after four hundred years in bondage, they were resistant to change, preferring the known hardships to the unknown trails in the desert leading them to freedom.

Or consider being in an abusive and toxic relationship: Mustering the courage and strength to break free, you finally escape its suffocating grip. At first, the newfound freedom fills you with hope and relief, like you've got your life back. Yet, soon, the reality of being single sinks in, and loneliness creeps in. You are unable to find that special someone. In this desperate state, instead of patiently waiting at the red light, trusting in God's timing for a healthier relationship, you find yourself tempted to return to the familiar but harmful embrace of your past. How many of us have been ensnared by this cycle? I've witnessed several individuals succumb to this temptation, often rationalizing their decision with excuses.

4. **The red light is not your destination**; it's just a pause: We've explored various facets of the stoplight metaphor, yet the most challenging aspect is not mistaking a pause for our final destination. It's common to feel during prolonged waits that the delay is endless, and we're tempted to become resigned to our fate as if there's no way out. This perception, however, doesn't reflect

reality. As long as you have breath and clarity of thought, your journey is not over.

The stoplight in our lives assumes different forms for each of us. For some, it's the wait for the love of your life. For others, a much-anticipated job promotion. It could manifest as a period of imprisonment or time spent bedridden in a hospital. These pauses are not indications of permanence but rather moments of preparation. They remind us that God orchestrates our journeys through different seasons, assuring us that the green light will shine when the timing is perfect.

Bethany Hamilton, a professional surfer from Hawaii, is one person who has experienced these stoplights. When she lost her left arm to a tiger shark at the age of 13, she might have felt like her whole life was lost. She could have viewed it as her fate and given up on her passion and dream career. She could have felt like a victim, even though she was a survivor of the tragedy, and relied on other people to take care of her.

However, Bethany refused to view this pause as her ultimate destination. Within just 26 days of the incident, she was back on her surfboard, challenging the waves and her own limits. This period of a forced red light wasn't her destination; it was a brief interlude in her remarkable journey.

Her triumph over adversity didn't stop at getting back on the board; she went on to win her first national surfing title within two years of the attack. Bethany's ability to not only return to surfing but also excel at it demonstrates the incredible power of faith, perseverance, and courage to move towards her destination. She allowed God to work through her circumstances, transforming what many would see as a tragic end into a powerful beginning.

Bethany became a beacon of hope and inspiration, showing that the red lights we encounter are not our final destinations but opportunities for growth and testimonies of faith. She turned her experience into a blessing for others and exemplified that, with faith, determination, and courage, we can move forward, no matter the obstacles we face.

Her website shares the following about her incredible journey: "Bethany has been able to touch a large number of people with her faith message, charitable efforts, and overall spirit. Her greatest joy is being a wife and mother, and Bethany continues to touch and inspire lives globally as a professional surfer, author and motivational speaker. She currently has her own blog and online course, along with a mother daughter mentorship program called the 'Ohana Experience, all centered on helping young women be unstoppable in life and faith."[1]

The Bible offers a few more examples of people who had to pause at a red light because they hadn't reached their destination yet:
1. Abraham and Sarah: They waited about 25 years for the fulfillment of God's promise of a son, Isaac *(Genesis 12:4; 21:5)*.
2. Joseph: Sold into slavery by his brothers, Joseph spent years in Potiphar's house and in prison before rising to prominence in Egypt—a process that took over 13 years *(Genesis 37–41)*.
3. Moses: He spent 40 years in the desert of Midian as a shepherd before God called him to lead the Israelites out of Egypt *(Acts 7:29–30)*.

4. The Israelites: They wandered in the desert for 40 years before entering the Promised Land *(Numbers 14:33–34)*.
5. Simeon and Anna: Both were elderly and had been waiting for the Messiah. Simeon had been promised he would not die before seeing the Lord's Christ. Both met Jesus when He was presented at the temple as a baby *(Luke 2:25–38)*.
6. The apostles and early disciples: After Jesus' ascension, they waited in Jerusalem for the coming of the Holy Spirit, which occurred on Pentecost, 50 days after Jesus' resurrection *(Acts 1:4–5; 2:1–4)*.
7. Paul: After his conversion, Paul spent several years in Damascus, Arabia, and Tarsus before beginning his public ministry *(Galatians 1:17–18; Acts 9:19–30; 11:25–26)*.

In life, God allows us to encounter several red lights to develop our patience. This development of patience is essential for strengthening our faith and trust in God's timing. While it might seem unfair or even unnecessary to endure these experiences, they are vital for drawing us closer to God and preparing us for what is to come when the light turns green.

In the grand scheme of things, everything will make perfect sense, but since we can't see the full picture at the moment, we often fail to understand. Therefore, it's wiser and safer to entrust all possibilities to God and wait for His timing.

Can you even fathom the thought that Jesus waited four thousand years to be born on this earth? It's a compelling illustration of divine timing over human impatience. From a human perspective, it might seem logical for Jesus to have come earlier, perhaps as Adam and Eve's firstborn, to set an example for living a sinless life right from humanity's inception. However, this viewpoint assumes that the timing of Jesus' birth is solely about combating sin in its early stages, rather than the culmination of a much larger divine plan.

The suggestion that God waited for sin to develop to a terrible point before sending Jesus might seem to imply a certain willingness on God's part to see humanity suffer, but this interpretation misses the broader theological context. Unfortunately, many people choose to rely on flawed human concepts rather than seeking to directly understand the workings of God.

The wait for Jesus' coming, then, can be seen not as a delay or a desire to witness suffering but as a strategic moment in God's plan of salvation for humanity. It serves as a reminder that God's perspective is vastly different from ours, encompassing not only the immediate but the eternal. Our struggles to be patient and understand God's timing are part of our human condition, yet they also offer opportunities for growth in faith and trust.

While we don't possess all the details of why Jesus came four thousand years after the creation of the world, we have insights into some significant reasons:

1. The enormity of sin: According to the parable of the wheat and tares *(Matthew 13:24–30, 36–43)*, God allowed sin to fully develop to demonstrate the distinction between the righteous and the sinful. This lesson extends beyond our world, offering insights to the universe at large, which includes other worlds observing and learning from our experiences.
2. The fulfillment of prophecies: By the time of Jesus' arrival on the earth, there were three hundred prophecies about Him. Through His birth, life, death, resurrection,

and ascension to heaven, He fulfilled all these prophecies, establishing Himself as the most credible figure in human history. These fulfillments leave little room for doubt among those sincerely seeking to understand Christ.

3. The fullness of time: The New Testament says that Jesus came in the "fullness of the time" *(Galatians 4:4)*, indicating that His arrival was meticulously planned within God's sovereign timeline. This timing was likely optimal due to various factors, such as geopolitical conditions, cultural readiness, and the infrastructure of the Roman Empire, which facilitated the spread of the gospel.

4. In Christian understanding, the arrival of Jesus in the fullness of time—as described in *Galatians 4:4*—was not just about addressing sin but also about revealing the depth of God's love, grace, and redemption to a world fully entangled in sin's grasp. This timing reflects a pivotal moment in divine history, in which God's intervention through Christ's life, death, and resurrection would have the maximum impact on humanity's relationship with Him.

5. The preparation of humanity: Some theologians suggest that humanity needed time to understand its need for a savior. By allowing history to unfold and human civilization to develop, God prepared the way for Jesus' arrival. Through the experiences of the Israelites, the teachings of the prophets, and the moral development of various cultures, people became more receptive to the message of salvation Jesus offered.

> *"God isn't just observing the earth from millions of miles away; He is actively involved in our daily lives, experiencing each moment alongside us."*

Some may argue that waiting four thousand years was easy for Jesus because, according to *2 Peter 3:8*, a thousand years is like a day in heaven. However, it's important to remember that God isn't just observing the earth from millions of miles away; He is actively involved in our daily lives, experiencing each moment alongside us.

In essence, the narrative of waiting in the Bible—from the prophets anticipating the Messiah to the apostles awaiting the Holy Spirit—teaches us about the value of divine timing. It reassures us that God is at work even in the wait, working all things together for good for those who love Him *(Romans 8:28)*. Thus, while we may not always understand all the reasons behind our red lights, we are encouraged to trust in God's overarching plan and timing, confident that He is sovereign and that His plans for us are for our ultimate good.

Furthermore, consider our own experiences: When we love someone deeply, we feel their pain acutely. How much more, then, does our Creator—Jesus—suffer with us? He longs to rescue us from this world marred by sin, yet He had to wait for the perfect moment to enter our world. He was born into it as an innocent baby. He lived righteously, died a terrible death, and triumphed in resurrection. Now, if Jesus could wait thousands of years to take us to heaven, to eradicate sin from the universe, and to end all pain, suffering, and death for eternity, can't we also wait a few years for a better life and a better eternity?

> *"Wait on the LORD; be of good courage, and He shall strengthen your heart; wait, I say, on the LORD!"* (Psalm 27:14)

Patience with People

I watched a video of a couple who brought a stray dog into their home. The dog looked unkempt and would growl and try to bite whenever someone attempted to touch it. So, they allowed the dog to gradually get used to their presence. Eventually, they were able to hold the dog, reassuring it that they meant no harm. It took weeks for the couple to fully groom the dog—bathing it, trimming its hair, and cutting its nails.

Even though in the beginning, the dog growled and tried to bite, over time, it grew increasingly comfortable with their touch and enjoyed being cleaned and fed. In the end, the video showed the dog, with its coat beautifully regrown and even, running around the house and playing with the couple, who are now its owners. The dog no longer felt threatened nor posed a threat to them. It was not only a moving video but also a thought-provoking lesson.

Isn't this similar to how people are when they enter our lives? We don't know their backgrounds, their traumas, their weaknesses, their struggles, their insecurities, or their fears. Whether they become our friends, relatives, or colleagues, they bring their personal experiences with them. Just like the couple didn't get upset with the dog for growling or attempting to bite, we shouldn't take it personally when someone makes an unkind comment or offends us. Often, these actions aren't personal but rather a reflection of past issues they are still carrying with them. Our role here is to be patient and show kindness to them as God has shown His patience to us:

> *"The Lord is not slack concerning His promise, as some count slackness, but is longsuffering [patient] toward us, not willing that any should perish but that all*

should come to repentance. ... And consider that the longsuffering [patience] of our Lord is salvation—as also our beloved brother Paul, according to the wisdom given to him, has written to you" (2 Peter 3:9, 15, emphasis added).

These verses from *2 Peter* highlight God's incredible patience and longsuffering towards humanity, despite our sins and shortcomings. As recipients of God's patience, we are called to extend the same patience to others, particularly those who may offend us or cause trouble.

Patience with people involves understanding that everyone has their own journey and struggles, and not everyone will behave or respond in the way we expect or desire. Just as God patiently waits for us to turn to Him in repentance, we should extend grace, understanding, and patience to others as they navigate their own paths.

Furthermore, as the couple patiently worked with the dog, never giving up despite its initial resistance, their persistent care and choice to not take the dog's anger personally helped transform their relationship gradually. Over time, it blossomed into something beautiful and thriving. Likewise, demonstrating patience with others creates opportunities for growth and reconciliation. This approach provides the space needed for forgiveness and allows relationships to heal and flourish.

By embodying God's patience and longsuffering, we not only reflect His character but also foster a more compassionate and harmonious community. Jesus exemplified this when He prayed for His enemies, saying, *"Father, forgive them, for they do not know what they do" (Luke 23:34).* It's crucial to seek God's perspective, see others with compassion, and pray for them. Instead of taking things personally or feeling victimized, we should ask God to help us mature in our faith, enabling us to extend His love and compassion even towards those who may harm us or whom we perceive as enemies.

Patience is most needed when we face challenging people. Isn't it easy for us to pet a dog that is loving, wants belly rubs, and poses no harm to us? But we need to be patient with the dog that threatens us, especially if it's a part of our life. Similarly, we might have challenging people in our workplace, church, hospital, neighborhood, or family. Despite challenges like hurtful words or betrayal, having patience showcases love and grace and reveals the worth of each individual.

You might find it challenging to maintain patience, but in moments of frustration or impatience, remember the words of *Ephesians 4:2: "with all lowliness and gentleness, with longsuffering, bearing with one another in love."* May we continually strive to reflect the love and mercy of our heavenly Father. Can you think of a time when someone else was patient with you when you caused them trouble?

Indeed, while patience and understanding are essential aspects of Christian character, we have to recognize that they don't condone ongoing abuse or mistreatment from others. Jesus Himself advocated for setting healthy boundaries and seeking reconciliation when possible, but also withdrawing from harmful situations when necessary.

In situations where others persistently offend or abuse us, we need to prioritize our own well-being and safety. This may involve distancing ourselves from toxic relationships, seeking support from trusted friends or family members, or even seeking professional help or intervention when warranted. If that dog in the video hadn't shown any improvements in its behavior and had continued to pose a threat for weeks and months—or if it had even attacked the owners—the course of action from the owners would've been different.

Setting boundaries doesn't mean withholding forgiveness or harboring resentment; rather, it means recognizing our own dignity and worth as children of God and taking proactive steps to protect ourselves from harm and not enable unhealthy, toxic behaviors. By doing so, we demonstrate self-respect and model healthy relationships for others.

Ultimately, our goal as Christians should be to cultivate patience, which promotes a peaceful environment. However, we must also recognize our limitations and acknowledge that there are times when removing ourselves from harmful situations is the most prudent course of action.

Let's look at an instance when Jesus removed Himself from a harmful situation: *"Jesus said to them, 'Most assuredly, I say to you, before Abraham was, I AM.' Then they [the Pharisees] took up stones to throw at Him; but Jesus hid Himself and went out of the temple, going through the midst of them, and so passed by"* (John 8:58–59).

In all things, let's seek wisdom and guidance from God, who promises to lead us on paths of righteousness and provide strength, comfort, and patience in times of trial.

The Hardest Person to Be Patient With

You! Yes, you have the least patience with yourself. Below are some aspects for you to evaluate and work on in your own life:

1. **Self-criticism:** While self-criticism can be constructive if it leads to personal growth, many people tend to be overly critical of themselves. They set unrealistic standards and experience frustration or disappointment when they don't meet them. For instance, imagine you receive a low grade on a test, or ask a question in a workshop that everyone else knows the answer to, or prepare a meal where one course has a bitter aftertaste. Instead of objectively analyzing what went wrong and how to improve next time, you conclude, "I'm so dumb, I just can't get anything right." This type of self-criticism is harmful because it generalizes a specific incident into an overarching judgment about your abilities and self-worth.

2. **Impatience with progress:** People often expect immediate results or rapid progress when working towards personal growth and development, such as learning a new skill or losing weight. When they don't see immediate progress as hoped, they become discouraged or impatient with themselves, overlooking the gradual nature of improvement. For example, when I was in the process of losing weight, I really was impatient and hard on myself. I didn't see my weight go down as rapidly as I wanted it to. I always reasoned that if my weight could increase 2–5 pounds overnight, then why couldn't it reduce that way? This mindset only added stress and made the weight loss journey even more challenging. However, once I learned proper weight loss techniques and adopted a patient approach, I began to see success. Patience proved essential for sustainable progress. Do

you struggle with impatience in something similar or in another aspect?

3. **Self-doubt:** Feelings of self-doubt or inadequacy lead people to constantly question their abilities or worth. This lack of self-assurance can lead to impatience with themselves because they may feel frustrated by perceived limitations or shortcomings. For instance, imagine receiving a compliment on a project you completed. Instead of accepting the compliment, you dismiss it, thinking the task was too simple, suspecting the compliment was just politeness, or believing others could have done it better. This inability to recognize your own value not only fuels further self-doubt and impatience but also prevents you from appreciating your own skills and contributions.

4. **Harsh self-comparison:** Comparing oneself unfavorably to others can fuel feelings of impatience and dissatisfaction. Let's say you recently joined the gym to improve your health and fitness. Instead of focusing on your personal progress, you berate yourself by comparing your fitness level and abilities to those of more experienced gym-goers. This harsh comparison distracts you from recognizing the improvements in your stamina and strength, ultimately causing you to be impatient and making your gym experience stressful rather than enjoyable.

"Every thought you tell yourself will either empower you or limit you."

5. **Difficulty accepting mistakes:** Many people find it challenging to accept their own mistakes or shortcomings, viewing them as personal failures rather than opportunities for learning and growth. This reluctance to embrace imperfection can contribute to impatience with oneself.

As my wife says, "Every thought you tell yourself will either empower you or limit you." Ask God to give you the strength to think positive things about yourself, know your self-worth, and change the way you see yourself. Then, you will see progress towards a better you.

> *"Be anxious for nothing, but in everything by prayer and supplication, with thanksgiving, let your requests be made known to God; and the peace of God, which surpasses all understanding, will guard your hearts and minds through Christ Jesus"* (Philippians 4:6–7).
>
> *"I can do all things through Christ who strengthens me"* (Philippians 4:13).

Reflections:

1. Are you waiting at a red light in your life right now? If yes, write down how long you are willing to wait and what emotions you are experiencing while waiting at the red light.
2. Now, write down how this waiting time can help you appreciate things when you finally achieve them.
3. How can you make the best out of this waiting time?
4. Write down a list of people whom you dislike. Take time to write a note or letter of gratitude to at least two people per week, listing genuine things you have observed about them that you are truly thankful for. Repeat this process until you exhaust the list. Doing so will help you develop patience with others.
5. Write down a list of issues you have with yourself that make you anxious and impatient. Now, imagine

QUALITY LIFE

that what you have written above is for your friend and not yourself. What suggestions would you give to this friend? Implement these suggestions in your own life.

6. Memorize two Bible promises that you can recite whenever you feel insecure about yourself.

References

1. "Learn About Bethany," Bethany Hamilton, bethanyhamilton.com/biography.

Chapter Four
KINDNESS
Developing A Gentle Spirit

During my three-year stay in Maine, I had the pleasure of having a wonderful couple, Brian and Carol, as my neighbors. In short, they were one of a kind. They generously shared their homegrown vegetables with me, and one spring, Carol offered me one of their extra bicycles to use until the fall season when Maine gets covered in a thick layer of snow.

I accepted their kind offer and used the bike for my evening exercise routine. Behind my house, past some train tracks, was a peaceful and welcoming neighborhood. Taking a left turn led to a paved path where people jogged, walked, and biked. It was a perfect spot for outdoor activities.

During my rides, I enjoyed observing children playing along the path—some were roller skating, while others were running, biking, or simply strolling with their families. On one side were houses, while on the other side flowed a river, its peaceful sound adding to the charm of the surroundings. Riding the bike in this setting was always a delight.

After my rides, I would park the bike on the first-floor porch near my landlord's office since my apartment was on the second floor. I never felt the need to lock the bike as I put it discreetly out of view from the street, facing Brian and Carol's house.

One morning, much to my surprise, my bike wasn't in its usual spot. I suspected my mischievous friend Jason of playing a prank on me since he was quite capable of such antics. When I contacted him, he denied being near my apartment. I wondered if other friends could have hidden my bike since very few besides my visitors or the landlord's clients knew its location.

As the sun was setting and I still had no word on my missing bike, I started to realize that the bike was actually stolen. Anxiety crept in, especially because the bike belonged to my dear friends. I grappled with how to break the news to them, knowing it was my oversight for not securing the bike. My heart felt heavy knowing that I lost the bike that had been lent to me. However, I resolved to inform my neighbors about the theft.

Sharing my plight with my landlord proved beneficial since the building was equipped with security cameras. He granted me access to review the footage, and as I watched, a chill ran down my spine at the sight of a figure entering the property around midnight—an entirely new feeling to me. The face was unfamiliar, but what caught my attention was the paint on his hands. I replayed the footage several times, observing how he made a beeline for the bike, pausing briefly to scan the surroundings and casting a glance toward my apartment. It became evident that this wasn't his first visit; he lifted the bike off the porch, descended the steps, and rode away into the night.

Part of me was furious and part of me felt like, I myself am a poor person. How could he steal the bike from me? Especially a bike lent to me? This incident brought back memories of my younger years when I had won a bike as a raffle prize back in India, only to have it stolen and never recovered. I was determined not to let history repeat itself. I knew I had to take some bold steps to track down the thief and reclaim the stolen bike.

But before that, I needed to inform Brian and Carol about what had happened and reassure them that by God's grace, we would find the bike soon. So, I finally mustered up the courage to tell them. Their reaction surprised me—instead of getting upset or questioning our friendship, they calmly acknowledged that such incidents occur and advised me to be cautious. I assured them that I would do everything in my power to locate the bike and return it to them.

I proceeded to the police station, where I made a report along with all the evidence I had gathered. The police officer seemed skeptical about my success, citing numerous cases of stolen bikes that were never recovered. Nonetheless, he assured me that he would make every effort to locate the bike. After returning home, I decided to search the nearby areas in hopes of spotting the bike or finding a lead. After considering several locations as potential hiding spots, I eventually made my way back home.

As I returned home, I noticed a police vehicle parked outside. It was the same officer I had reported the theft to. He showed me a picture of a bike and asked whether it matched my stolen bike. In disbelief, I confirmed that it was indeed mine and inquired about its recovery. The officer explained that a woman had reported a bike brought onto her property by a young man under her care, unsure if it was stolen. By cross-referencing our complaints, the officer was able to connect the dots.

We quickly went to the woman's residence. Seeing the bike in person lifted the heaviness off my heart. The woman, a medical professional, shared that she had provided shelter to a homeless young man until he found employment and could support himself. He had since started working for a construction company. As I reflected on the situation, I felt a sense of pride in deciphering a crucial detail—the presence of paint on the man's hands, which the woman confirmed.

She recounted how the young man had brought the bike one night and left it outside her house. When she questioned him, he claimed he found it unattended on a main road, about ten minutes from my apartment. He mentioned that it seemed abandoned, lying on the roadside. Skeptical of his story, she decided to report it to the police station in case someone reported a missing bike.

When I showed her the video captured by my landlord's camera, she confirmed he was the same individual who had stayed at her place. She also identified the paint on his hands from his job. With the case resolved, I happily retrieved my bike and headed home. It was a rewarding feeling to provide valuable clues that assisted law enforcement in recovering stolen property. With this remarkable resolution, I could return to my routine work.

But the story didn't end there.

True Kindness

I informed my neighbors that the bike had been found, and they were elated. An hour later, Brian visited my apartment and gave me a bike lock. He inquired about the whereabouts of the young thief, to which I informed him that the young man had not returned to the lady's house since the incident, and his current location remained unknown.

Brian's words at that moment made me realize what true kindness looked like. He said, "He stole the bike because perhaps the distance to work was too far for him to walk, and he wanted a bike to help with his commute. If you find out where he is staying or working now, please let me know. I have an extra bike, and I would like to give it to him. He shouldn't have to steal from others when he can have his own."

These words of kindness have changed my perspective on what true kindness means. Why would someone want to show kindness to a thief? Shouldn't we, on the contrary, punish the person immediately for their wrongdoing?

> "kindness is not limited to supporting the poor and needy or helping those deemed "good people." It extends to aiding those who may have made mistakes or are considered "bad people.""

If someone has done wrong and they've been caught, shouldn't they be accused and seen as a bad person? Why do they even deserve kindness when they can't show kindness to others? What is kindness anyway?

Kindness entails showing compassion, empathy, and goodwill towards others. It involves acts of generosity, understanding, and consideration for people's feelings and well-being, often without expecting anything in return. Such acts may include helping the poor, providing medical support in third-world countries, building houses, or bringing fresh drinking water to the unfortunate.

While these are all true, kindness is not limited to supporting the poor and needy or helping those deemed "good people." It extends to aiding those who may have made mistakes or are considered "bad people." An often-overlooked aspect of kindness is guiding individuals away from wrongdoing and showing a better way of living by your example. It's compassion and understanding towards even those who may have fallen short. In this way, kindness is more inclusive and empathetic than we realize.

When someone makes a mistake, empathy—like what Brian showed—plays a crucial role. It involves understanding the circumstances and motivations behind the wrongdoer's actions. What led them to do wrong? How can they be supported and guided towards making better choices? Brian's willingness to offer a bike to the thief exemplifies this approach. By addressing the root cause of the thief's behavior and providing a positive alternative, Brian hopes to not only prevent further wrongdoing but also foster the thief's personal growth and integration into society.

Bad People in Society

In any given society, there are typically three types of individuals when it comes to wrongdoing:

1. Outright wrongdoing: These individuals consistently and intentionally engage in behavior that is harmful or unethical.
2. Circumstantial Wrongdoing: These individuals may find themselves in circumstances where they make poor choices or engage in wrongdoing, perhaps due to their actual needs, but they are held accountable when caught.
3. Undetected wrongdoing: These individuals may engage in harmful behavior without facing consequences or being detected by others or authorities.

Interestingly, the individuals of categories 1 and 3 are often the quickest to cast judgment on those of category 2. This dynamic reflects the complexities of human behavior and societal attitudes towards morality and accountability. Kindness is often missing.

A poignant illustration of this complexity can be found in the story of Mary Magdalene, as recounted in *John 8:1–11*. She was brought before Jesus by the scribes and Pharisees, who claimed she was caught in the act of adultery.

In His early ministry, Jesus explained that even looking at a woman inappropriately is equivalent to committing adultery with her in one's heart. Even so, He surprised the scribes and Pharisees by pointing the situation back to them, saying, *"He who is without sin among you, let him throw a stone at her first"* *(John 8:7)*. When the scribes and Pharisees left because of their own guilt, Jesus said to Mary Magdalene, *"Neither do I condemn you; go and sin no more" (John 8:11)*, choosing understanding and forgiveness over condemnation and judgment. This response conveyed a crucial lesson about the significance of compassion and refraining from judgment towards others. It's still a powerful testament to the transformative nature of kindness.

Later, when Mary showed repentance by anointing Jesus' feet with expensive oil, she faced condemnation from Judas Iscariot—a reflection of his own moral shortcomings. He criticized her for using the costly oil to anoint Jesus instead of selling it to give the proceeds to the poor. Judas condemned her not out of concern for the poor but because of his own greed because he was known to steal from the money box he was in charge of *(John 12:6)*.

While Mary's circumstances leading to adultery remain unclear, what we do see is that throughout Jesus' ministry, the scribes and Pharisees acted wrong outright. Exploiting their power, they sought to trap Jesus rather than genuinely address the situation.

These scenarios reveal the three types of wrongdoers. The scribes and Pharisees represent outright wrongdoing. Mary exemplifies circumstantial wrongdoing that was exposed. And Judas embodies undetected wrongdoing. The Bible condemns Judas, yet those around him didn't truly know who he was, except for Jesus, who is the *"discerner of the thoughts and intents of the heart" (Hebrews 4:12).*

God's Kindness

Through Mary Magdalene's story, we glean a profound lesson: Jesus extended forgiveness to individuals from all three categories—the scribes and Pharisees, Mary Magdalene, and Judas Iscariot. Rather than making sure they received retribution for their various wrongdoings, whether overt or covert, Jesus chose kindness.

To everyone who has ever done wrong, Jesus offers pardon and says, *"Go and sin no more" (John 8:11).* He has been doing this since the fall of Adam and Eve. Yet, His forgiveness isn't merely pardon; it comes with the provision for transformative change.

What are the provisions He has for us? The fact that there are so many demonstrates the depth of His kindness:
1. Grace and mercy: Jesus offers us the gift of salvation through His sacrificial death on the cross and His resurrection. Despite our shortcomings and sins, He forgives

us, gives us a new beginning, and helps us make better choices. By placing our faith in Him and accepting His sacrifice for our sins, we are reconciled with God and granted eternal life.

2. The Holy Spirit: Jesus promised to send the Holy Spirit to dwell within us and guide and empower us to live a life pleasing to God. The Holy Spirit convicts us of our sins, leads us into the truth, and enables us to live transformed lives.

3. The Word of God: Jesus gives us the gift of His Word, the Bible, which is a light in darkness to show us the right path and has the power to recreate in us a new heart. By studying and applying His teachings, we gain wisdom, insight into His character, and an understanding of God's will for our lives.

4. Fellowship and community: Jesus established a Christian community of believers to support, strengthen, encourage, and hold one another accountable in the journey of faith.

5. Prayer: Jesus taught us to pray and communicate with God regularly. Prayer allows us to seek guidance, confess our sins, and receive the strength and wisdom we need to live godly lives. The amazing part of this communication is, we can share all our deepest feelings and concerns openly with Him, the same way we would share with a father, mother, or best friend. Jesus tells us, just as He told Mary Magdalene: *"Neither do I condemn you: go and sin no more" (John 8:11)*. He is ever willing to help us out of our mistakes rather than condemn us.

6. His example: Jesus lived a perfect, sinless life as an example for us. He came to live our story, to empathize with our weaknesses, but He was victorious and thus able to help us. Studying His life and understanding that He identifies

with us can be a source of strength and comfort. As we surrender daily and moment by moment, He is willing to take all of what we are, and He will give all of who He is so we can live a life filled with His character. Jesus in us renews us.

Ultimately, through the forgiveness and provisions that Jesus has made for us, He demonstrates His unfathomable love and desire for our spiritual well-being. He desires not only our forgiveness but also our transformation into His likeness. By embracing God's kindness, we can experience true freedom and the highest quality of life in Him.

Our Kindness

The kindness God has shown us doesn't stop with us. It's our responsibility to also offer this kindness to others, following the example set by Jesus. If God has forgiven us and created opportunities for us to improve ourselves— for our own benefit and the benefit of others and society as a whole—then it's necessary for us to forgive others and help them find their path towards a better quality of life.

Kindness, synonymous with gentleness, encompasses the qualities of sympathy and empathy. While it comes naturally to extend these virtues to loved ones and even strangers at times, the challenge is extending them to our enemies, those who have wronged us, or those we've deemed bad. However, true kindness involves having mercy for everyone, even in the face of adversity, just like Jesus had.

Nevertheless, extending mercy doesn't mean overlooking or

enabling wrongdoing. We must discern between those who engage in wrongdoing out of necessity and those who do so out of power, arrogance, or intention. While we may empathize with those in dire circumstances, we can't condone deliberate acts of harm.

Indeed, there's a profound difference between showing kindness to those who make mistakes and offering them opportunities for improvement versus enabling or excusing purposeful wrongdoing. Striking this balance requires a nuanced understanding of human behavior and a commitment to upholding justice while also fostering compassion and understanding.

However, kindness is to be shown to everyone, regardless of the category they fall into. Those who engage in outright wrongdoing deserve justice, but the justice given should be tempered with kindness, providing them with the opportunity to rise higher from their current state and lead a changed life. When we are the affected party, extending kindness can be difficult but not impossible.

This is where God's provision comes in. As we surrender our lives to Christ and let Him live in and through us, He will produce the kindness we need.

Just as Brian was willing to give the thief a different bike so that he wouldn't have to steal again, we can show kindness to someone who has wronged us. In our own strength, it may seem impossible, but we "can do all things through Christ who strengthens" us (Philippians 4:13). This enables us to live the best quality of life while also providing a way for others to do the same.

> *"May the Lord make you increase and abound in love to one another and to all ... so that He may establish your hearts blameless in holiness before our God and Father at the coming of our Lord Jesus Christ with all His saints"* (1 Thessalonians 3:12–13).

Reflections:
1. Write down a list of past situations in which you could have shown kindness to someone.
2. List at least five different instances when others have shown you kindness or empathy even though you didn't treat them well.
3. How does God's kindness to you inspire you to be kind to others? List the ways God has shown His kindness to you, even when you were in the wrong.

—◆—

Chapter Five

VIRTUE

Essence of Time Well Spent

◆✦◆

Virtue is the essence of time well spent. While various dictionaries define virtue primarily as a standard of morality, whether objective or subjective, it is not confined to this realm alone. Morality is typically understood as the distinction between right and wrong, good and bad behavior, and the choice to pursue right and good actions, thus enabling a harmonious society. Basically, morality is a standard established as a social construct. However, virtue extends beyond mere morality.

Virtue reflects goodness in all aspects of character that are nurtured within the heart, whether someone is watching or not, and regardless of its impact on others. Many Christians would relate virtue to *Proverbs 31*, which speaks of a virtuous woman. If you read the entire chapter, you will notice that it doesn't focus solely on the woman's morality but much more.

Proverbs 31:10–31 describes a virtuous individual as someone who is trustworthy, hardworking, resourceful, diligent, strong, wise, generous, kind, skillful, fearless, elegant, compassionate, energetic, prudent, dignified, organized, respected, supportive, optimistic, self-disciplined, honorable, industrious, attentive, intelligent, confident, and faithful.

Virtue isn't an external display but a clear decision that starts from an internal experience. Virtue is how we live our life, and how we live our life is related to how we spend our time. At its core, virtue involves using our time wisely in a consistent way. This commitment to goodness isn't just about outward appearances or behavior in front of others; it reflects a deep-seated integrity that resides within the heart. True virtue is cultivated in the heart, guiding us to live rightly even when no one else is watching.

> *"Virtue is how we live our life, and how we live our life is related to how we spend our time."*

So, how do we cultivate this virtue? This journey begins with first understanding God's virtuous character. Then, by rooting our morals and principles in God, we ensure that they are not shaken or compromised in any circumstances. By consistently choosing goodness, even when it's challenging, we spend our time wisely. As a result, we develop the virtuous character that aligns with the goodness of God.

As we grow in virtue, we not only improve our own lives but also positively impact those around us, fostering a world where goodness prevails. Remember, *"all things work together for good" (Romans 8:28)* when we entrust them to God. Strive to allow God to live His virtuous life through you, and you will find yourself making the most of your time and living a quality life *(Galatians 2:20)*.

Understanding God's Virtue

Why isn't the virtue or goodness of God stopping people from destruction or pain? Because we live in a world of sin, ruled by Satan's vicious plans, we are affected by him both directly and indirectly. Some may choose to reject God and live according to Satan's plan, thus allowing Satan control of their lives. But when we bring our pain, hurt, abuse, and trauma to the infinite God who sees the big picture we can't see, He uses them for a greater good.

But for what greater good? If only God were to destroy Satan, his angels, and his followers right away, then we would have everlasting peace, and that would be the greater good, wouldn't it? Not really. If God operated in that manner, you and I would cease to exist the moment we committed a sin, even when we told our first lie as children.

God will ultimately destroy Satan and his followers, but before that He also wants to save as many people as possible to be with Him in the heavenly mansions. He is so virtuous that He cares for the wicked as much as He cares for the righteous. If God convicts you of your sins, don't you think you need a little more time to make things right with Him? I know I honestly do. Likewise, He gives time for the wicked to repent.

The Bible says God is not a respecter of persons, which means He is not partial or biased *(Romans 2:11)*. Did you ever think of the depth of that? God sustains everyone and everything equally as *Matthew 5:45* notes: *"He [God] makes His sun rise on the evil and on the good, and sends rain on the just and on the unjust."* Only a God who loves every single creation of His would sustain them like that. If He didn't love them, why would He want to sustain them?

If you ever have trails and hardships, reach out to this God of virtue and you will see your sincere prayers being answered in different ways and times. These answers might not be the way you expect but they will be for your best. If you haven't reached out to this virtuous God yet, I encourage you to try Him.

For those who do not know God, yet still reach out for help when they realize their own limitations, have experienced His assistance. Their cries, though not directed with a specific knowledge of God, are still heard, and they have been helped or protected by Him. This shows the virtuous character of God.

Many individuals have shared about their encounters with God during tough times. Unfortunately, these testimonies often go unnoticed, and we tend to focus solely on the negative aspects, portraying God in a negative light. It's crucial to remember that God is always present and willing to help.

While pain and suffering are the consequences of someone obeying the enemy and making wrong choices, God still uses those consequences to help us grow. He turns our trials into opportunities to give hope, inspire, embolden, and bless others. God sees the bigger picture and desires to save both you and me even when we don't see the big picture.

Example of God's Virtue

In the book of Job, chapters one and two, we observe an interesting exchange between God and Satan. God directs Satan's attention to His follower Job, asking, *"Have you considered My servant Job, that there is none like him on the earth, a blameless and upright man, one who fears God and shuns evil?" (Job 1:8)*

Satan responds that Job's devotion stems from God's abundant blessings and the protective hedge around him and all that belongs to him. Satan challenges that if God were to remove all the protection, then Job would curse God.

So, God grants Satan permission: *"Behold, all that he has is in your power; only do not lay a hand on his person" (Job 1:12)*. As a result, Satan inflicts severe losses upon Job. He loses his livestock, servants, and even his beloved children.

Despite the unimaginable grief, Job remains steadfast. He tears his robe, shaves his head, and falls to the ground, worshiping God and blessing His name. *"In all this Job did not sin nor charge God with wrong" (Job 1:22)*.

The conversation between God and Satan continues, with Satan suggesting, *"Skin for skin! Yes, all that a man has he will give for his life. But stretch out Your hand now, and touch his bone and his flesh, and he will surely curse You to Your face!" (Job 2:4–5)*

God gives a little more permission to Satan, saying, *"Behold, he is in your hand, but spare his life" (Job 2:6)*.

Satan inflicts Job with painful boils from the sole of his foot to the crown of his head. But Job refuses to curse God, even when his wife urges him to. Instead, he maintains his integrity, recognizing that both blessings and trials come from God's hand.

We can learn several lessons from this passage, but our focus is on the virtuous character of God and the vicious character of Satan. God neither destroys nor afflicts His children. On the other hand, Satan is happy to cause destruction equally on all humanity and put the blame on the God of virtue *(Job 1:16)*.

Consider these thoughts: 1) Satan tempts God twice in this incident. First, he challenges God to destroy everything that Job possesses *(Job 1:11)*. The second time, he asks God to afflict Job's health *(Job 2:5)*. On both occasions, God didn't touch Job for destruction but gave Satan opportunities to correct himself from destroying God's creation. This clearly differentiates God's virtue from Satan's vicious character.

2) If God had to grant Satan permission to test His beloved Job, then Satan lacks the power to override God and harm any living creature without God's consent. In other words, we can conclude that Satan hasn't destroyed every single human being on the earth because he lacks permission from God. Take a moment to contemplate this idea. Are you able to fathom the magnitude of God's virtuous character?

We understand that God is the Creator, the Protector, and the ultimate bringer of justice. However, His role as our God goes beyond these aspects. He also extends His virtue to the preservation of all things, whether related to our fallen world or the unfallen realms. God is personally involved in every aspect, every single second, ensuring that His presence and care are constantly at work.

God's Virtue in Preservation

Most of the time, we fail to recognize God as the preserver or sustainer. His sustaining work is not occasional or only when there's a need; it is constant and ongoing. God didn't just create us and then leave us to fend for ourselves. Instead, He remains actively involved in our lives, continually providing His presence and care. Thus, we understand that God's virtue is not just an outward appearance of protection from evil but an inward preservation. This is because He holds every part of His creation near to His heart.

Nehemiah eloquently explains that God alone created the heaven, the heaven of heavens and their hosts, the earth and everything on it, as well as the seas and all that dwells within them (Nehemiah 9:6). Furthermore, he asserts that God not only created all things but also preserves them all. God preserves every single creation on the earth and in heaven. Several verses in Psalm 104 speak about God's sustaining power, too. I recommend you read it before you continue reading this chapter.

The following passages also speak about God's preservation:
"The heavens declare the glory of God; and the firmament shows His handiwork" (Psalm 19:1).

"Lift up your eyes on high, and see who has created these things, who brings out their host by number;

He calls them all by name, by the greatness of His might and the strength of His power; not one is missing" (Isaiah 40:26).

"Who covers the heavens with clouds, who prepares rain for the earth, who makes grass to grow on the mountains. He gives to the beast its food, and to the young ravens that cry" (Psalm 147:8–9).

"Who executes justice for the oppressed, who gives food to the hungry. The LORD gives freedom to the prisoners" (Psalm 146:7).

"In Him we live and move and have our being, as also some of your own poets have said, 'For we are also His offspring'" (Acts 17:28).

If God were not the preserver of all that He created, imagine the havoc the devil would have wreaked over the millennia, for the devil walks about like a roaring lion, seeking whom he may devour *(1 Peter 5:8)*. In *Matthew 10:30–31*, Jesus emphasizes that God knows every minute detail about us and that if He takes care of every single sparrow, then how much more valuable are we to Him.

Absolutely no one, whether in heaven or on earth, including us, has inherent power to sustain themselves. The air that blows, the sun that shines, the water that flows, the food that grows, the shelter to rest, and the health that is sustained are all given by the Most High. We can claim ownership of none of it.

Now you might wonder, But I work hard, earn money, and buy all my necessities, such as food, a house, and a car, etc. But tell me this, who germinated a seed into a plant that provides you with food or clothing or into a tree that provides wood? Who produces air and water for all the beings to use? Who created gravity so that we aren't just floating around in space and being hindered from accomplishing our day-to-day activities? How come gravity is only on the earth and not in outer space? Who separated the earth with gravity from outer space which has no gravity?

Who causes the earth to rotate to give us enough sunlight for existence and sustenance of life? How is the earth able to revolve perfectly around the sun and not collide with any other planets? If no one created anything that moves at a specific speed and pattern without any external force, then how has the earth done so to give us the same number of seconds, minutes, hours, days, weeks, months, and years for centuries? This means we don't have control over the environment as a whole. We are just using what has been provided for us.

Let's get a little more personal. Who is causing your heart to beat? Who is causing your lungs to exchange carbon dioxide for oxygen? Who is causing your kidneys to filter blood? Imagine your cells' function. Are you manually causing them to function? Can you metabolize the food into energy? No! Who is making mitochondria generate the energy you need? Do you see my point?

Apply the same principle to every single thing in this world. Without God behind the scenes, nothing works. We can't claim credit for any of these functions. We can't bring ourselves into existence, and we can't stop ourselves from dying. The only thing we can do is keep these organs healthy by feeding them what they need while we are alive.

> **When we dig deep into the core of things, we are just using everything that is already present. We never have and never will be able to bring something into existence out of nothing. To do that is a God thing!**

And unfortunately, we often use what we do have in our control for destruction—either of ourselves or others.

Yet even with our poor decisions, God sustains our every breath, every heartbeat, and every second we spend. If God were to withdraw His sustaining power, Satan would destroy every living creature. This shows the virtuous character of God. He doesn't slumber or sleep *(Psalm 121:4)*. He's a personal God who cares for us, protects us, and sustains us every single second and yet has given us free will regardless of the decisions we make.

On the contrary, Satan wants us to believe that we lack free will. He seeks to force and destroy us. Throughout the Bible, we observe how Satan employs various methods, including warfare, spiritual conflict, deception, temptation, accusation, oppression, possession, division, and more in his efforts to harm humanity. He doesn't like anything that he sees, whether animate or inanimate, because it reminds him of a creator God who is bigger than him. Thus, Satan is on a quest to destroy everything.

Satan hates all things equally, but for humans, he has an extra level of hatred, stemming from the fact that we are all created in the image of God *(Genesis 1:27)*. Oh, how he would love to destroy us all! While the Bible doesn't directly attribute these actions to Satan, several instances in the Bible show how he worked through people to try to harm or kill children and newborn babies. These incidents are in *Exodus 1:8–22, Esther 3:8–13, and Matthew 2:16–18*.

How easy it has become to destroy lives, whether through missiles, guns, oppression, bullying, or even the termination of a pregnancy. In Chennai, India, around 1986, a husband had an affair with another woman, leading him to be angry when he learned about his wife's pregnancy. After berating his wife in public, she decided to seek an abortion.

With a heavy heart, she went to a clinic near her house and asked the doctor to perform the abortion. The doctor agreed and made three attempts, but all of them failed. The doctor returned to the wife and told her that she was unable to perform the abortion, something that had never happened before in her experience. She explained that many young girls come for abortions and leave without any complications, but this case felt different. She believed that perhaps it was a sign from God that this child was meant to be born. She firmly stated that she wouldn't attempt the procedure again but suggested finding a different clinic if the wife still wanted to proceed.

Of course, the husband was skeptical of this unexpected turn of events. However, decades later, I can confidently thank God for preserving my life. I appreciate that He protected and preserved me, making me believe that there is a purpose for my existence. He has a purpose for every single child who is conceived. Knowing that He saved me because of His virtuous character, I strive to live a virtuous life by submitting to God's will.

Can We Be Virtuous Even in Tough Times?

How many times has God used a very bad situation for greater good? Joseph's situation is one of many examples. As a 17-year-old boy *(Genesis 37:2)*, he was the favorite child of his father and well taken care of. But in one day, his brothers changed his fate and sold him into captivity. He ended up in Egypt as a slave. Bitter tears, a terrified heart, and an unknown future became his reality. This experience transformed a pampered child into a mature man in a hurry.

Joseph, in his misery, chose to stay faithful to his father Jacob's God. He developed high moral values for himself. He was sincere and upright in his job. Even though he was exposed to several temptations at different times, he remained virtuous through it all. It would have been hard for Joseph to see a blessing in all this, but he used his time to be faithful in God's sight, and God in turn blessed him with favor and wisdom.

At the age of 30, Joseph was given another opportunity to work for God by interpreting two dreams for Pharaoh. As a result, Pharaoh appointed him as the governor of the land of Egypt. After getting married, Joseph named his firstborn child Manasseh, which means *"making forgetful."* He explained that God had made him forget his troubles and his father's household *(Genesis 41:51)*. Additionally, he named his second-born Ephraim, which means *"fruitfulness."* He expressed his gratitude to God for making him fruitful in the land of his suffering *(Genesis 41:52)*. These names serve as evidence that Joseph had forgiven his family and was thankful for the blessings he had received.

At the age of 39, Joseph once again encountered his brothers, the ones who had callously sold him while he pleaded in anguish. After subjecting them to a couple of tests, Joseph revealed his true identity. While the brothers were shocked to see their brother Joseph alive, he encouraged them not to feel guilty or angry with themselves for selling him into slavery. Even through all these ordeals as a slave for several years, Joseph used his time virtuously by being faithful to his God. When he saw his brothers, he didn't hold grudges against them. Now, this is the quality of life God wants us to have.

Joseph's wholehearted forgiveness is eloquently expressed in these words: *"And God sent me before you to preserve a posterity for you in the earth, and to save your lives by a great deliverance"* *(Genesis 45:7)*.

When Jacob, father of Joseph and his brothers, passed away, the brothers' guilt once again rose up as they wondered whether Joseph had left them alive because of their father. Joseph again assured them, *"'Do not be afraid, for am I in the place of God? But as for you, you meant evil against me; but God meant it for good, in order to bring it about as it is this day, to save many people alive. Now therefore, do not be afraid; I will provide for you and your little ones.' And he comforted them and spoke kindly to them"* (Genesis 50:19–21).

This response highlights the virtuous character of Joseph. He had once and for all forgiven his brothers for their cruel deed, closing that chapter for good. Joseph didn't perceive himself as a poor little slave but as the highest ruler next to Pharaoh in all the land of Egypt, the one in charge for a greater good. He understood that God had sent him to Egypt ahead of his family to preserve not only his own kin but also several hundred families during the seven-year famine. Joseph spent his life in submission to God, which allowed him to see the bigger picture of his trials and triumphs. Through this process, God developed a virtuous character in him. In other words, Joseph spent his time well. Can we, like Joseph, submit to God and allow Him to make us virtuous? Do we believe that even though our ancestors have been slaves and/or we have been subject to racial bigotry, caste, or any type of discrimination, God can still make us into a blessing to others? Do we believe God can make us into a blessing to the very same people that treated us unjustly, just like He did Joseph? The natural human tendency is to retaliate, take revenge, or feel like victims because of the evil done to us, but the virtue of God will lead us to do good in return for evil. Now that is virtue! Only a God of virtue can give us virtue for a quality life.

Time Travel or Virtue

Perhaps you're reading this chapter about virtue and feeling like you've messed up—you haven't lived according to Joseph's example. Maybe you even wish that you could travel back in time and live differently, embodying a virtuous character. Could we really go back in time to change our past into a virtuous one, paving the way for a better present? Let's explore the connection between time travel and virtue. But first, some intriguing facts about time travel.

The concept of time travel still remains a subject of debate among scientists. While some believe it to be merely a concept, others, like Einstein, believe it will become a reality someday. According to Einstein's theory of relativity, time and motion are relative to each other, and nothing can travel faster than the speed of light, which is 186,000 miles per second.

According to Einstein's theory of *"time dilation,"* time travel is not impossible. For instance, an object traveling at high speed is subject to time dilation and ages more slowly than a stationary object. This means that if you travel at high speeds in outer space and return, you could travel thousands of years into the future. However, traveling back to the past is not possible, despite what movies may portray. Furthermore, no invention has been discovered that allows travel at the speed of light. In addition, even if such an invention were to be created, the human body would disintegrate at the speed of 186,000 miles per second. Thus, it's unlikely to bring this concept into reality.

If only time travel were true, we could go back to the past, fix our mistakes, and make our present beautiful. For example, I could go back and stop myself from saying something foolish that hurt my wife. Thus, I could have avoided a big conflict between us.

Or if time travel were true, we could also travel to the future to understand our lives better and work in the present for a better future. I could go to the future and learn which type of currency will be predominantly used and then come back to the present to invest my money in that specific type of currency. Maybe I could even make an online course for people to learn about that currency, and I could make millions with it. Doesn't it seem like time travel would result in a peaceful and secure present?

But consider this: If we could travel back in time and correct our mistakes, wouldn't the temptation to fix our past blunders and make better choices be too great? And if that weren't enough, we'd be pulled by the lure of the future, constantly traveling back and forth in time to secure more wealth, power, and status. With all this, would we really be living in the present? Would we enjoy our relationships with our spouse, parents, children, and friends? Would we pause and appreciate the nature around us? Would we even see a need for God in our lives? While time travel sounds great, it's a huge blessing to know that it will never become reality.

Even so, how often we travel to the past and the future! What do I mean by this? We time travel in our minds, don't we? We often find ourselves traveling back to our past, dwelling on our own mistakes and regrets and allowing them to haunt us. If only I had another chance, we tell ourselves, I would make choices that I wouldn't regret later. The regret could be for any decision—a college major, a friend, a job, a romantic partner, a harmful habit, or something else. At the same time, we may also travel to the future with apprehension, feeling anxious about various aspects of life, such as raising our children, securing our financial situation, managing relationships, planning for retirement, or other concerns.

I want to encourage you that there is more to life than this type of time travel. God has forgiven our past mistakes however bad they might have been and has also given us a great hope for the future despite all the struggles life may throw at us. How can you say that? you may ask, and my response is, Look at the cross of calvary. Jesus' death reveals the ultimate forgiveness God has given us. Even if we are murderers, adulterers, pedophiles, thieves, etc., His death on the cross is enough to pardon all of it. You might even be part of a different religion, worshiping other gods, but this pardon is extended to anyone and everyone that lives on this earth. That is the virtue and goodness of God!

Often, past mistakes or negative experiences weigh us down and hinder us from looking at a hopeful future. Or there might be people constantly reminding us of our mistakes that can make us feel less. We may try to cope with these feelings in various ways, such as distracting ourselves, accepting them as our identity, or seeking outside support. However, true freedom is found in recognizing that through Christ, our past has been forgiven and our identity has been transformed. This realization allows us to embrace a hopeful future with renewed confidence. Jesus calls us, *"Come to Me, all you who labor and are heavy laden, and I will give you rest. Take My yoke upon you and learn from Me, for I am gentle and lowly in heart, and you will find rest for your souls. For My yoke is easy and My burden is light"* (Matthew 11:28–30).

Zacchaeus was an individual who experienced this gift. He was a chief tax collector but was viewed as a sinner because he unjustly took people's money. But when Jesus came to his home, Zacchaeus confessed his sins and promised to make his wrongs right. As a result, Jesus forgave him, changed his identity, and gave him hope for his future because salvation had come to his house. From then on, as long as Zacchaeus was faithful to Jesus, we will see him in heaven *(Luke 19:1–10)*. That is the virtue and goodness of God!

Virtue is the essence of time well spent, and constant worry or anxiety opposes such a life. To lead a virtuous life, we need to, like Zacchaeus, surrender our past, present, and future to Christ, being faithful to Him and acknowledging that He sees the big picture. Then, we will begin to realize that the goodness of God has been taking care of us all these years and will continue to do so. We might not have seen God's goodness taking care of us because we were busy time traveling in our minds. However, this doesn't change the fact that His virtue was there, even in our worst moments. That is the goodness of God!

Spending Time Virtuously

We are all gifted with the same amount of time each day—24 hours, no more, no less! The moment you wake up, life throws endless choices at you with every single step. It begins with deciding whether you want to rise immediately or hit the snooze button on your alarm and ends with your decision to go to bed right away or spend 15 more minutes on social media. These are just basic aspects of life, yet they have a critical influence on our well-being. They shape us into the people we become. They become our character.

Time is a precious commodity that never stops or waits for anyone. It can never be replenished once it's spent. We all know these facts, but what are we doing with this knowledge? Does it have a positive impact on us? Many people struggle, realizing they have lost a significant amount of time by failing to use it wisely. They may make these confessions on their death beds, after being in a coma, after being paralyzed, or simply when they feel they've been stuck in a rut for far too long. At some point in life, we need to recognize the importance of using our time wisely.

What does spending time wisely mean anyway? It means living purposefully and intentionally, making virtuous decisions. Goodness and virtue are used interchangeably. As we saw before, developing virtue is something that God has to work in and through us, but we make the decision to initiate that. Spending time with loved ones, pursuing a passion, taking a moment to appreciate the beauty of the nature around us, or taking time to reflect and connect with God are all virtuous decisions. By being mindful of how we spend our time and consciously choosing to prioritize what is important, we can live a life without regrets.

Always remember, every day, within those 24 hours, when we say yes to something, we are saying no to one or more things. Every thought we think, every single word we speak, every action we take, may it be virtuous in God's sight. Let's strive to always say yes to the right things as we are sustained by the God of virtue.

> *"See then that you walk circumspectly, not as fools but as wise, redeeming the time, because the days are evil" (Ephesians 5:15–16).*

Reflections:
1. Write down at least two times when someone has wronged you. Reflecting on the bigger picture, how do you see that these wrongs were ultimately used by God for a greater good? If you don't see it, ask God to show you.
2. Joseph, despite being a slave, remained virtuous. How does his example inspire you to pursue virtue regardless of your past or present situation?
3. Write down five instances you would handle differently if you were given another chance.
4. List three to five strategies you will use to avoid dwelling on past mistakes or worrying about the future.
5. Define in your own words how you would spend your time wisely.

—◆—

QUALITY LIFE

Chapter Six
HUMILITY
Who Is In Control?

Humility to Acknowledge God

Have you ever wished to be a superhero? Like Superman, Batman, Spiderman, Hancock, or some heroic character from Avengers or X-Men? I've admired a few. However, you would never see the phrase "based on a true story" in any of these movies. That's because none of these characters actually exist; they are just fictional fantasies. It's not uncommon for people to fantasize about possessing superhuman abilities or to imagine that there is something out there that will help them unlock their powers. Wondering about the possibilities beyond our ordinary experiences is a natural part of human imagination and curiosity.

Do you believe you can push yourself beyond your limits and maintain good health and quality of life, even with little sleep and constant overwork? In a sense, you are believing you are a superman or a superwoman.

People like Amy Carlson (the mother god), Sun Myung Moon, Sai Baba, and many others called themselves gods, yet none have risen from the dead to substantiate their claims. They lacked the supernatural power to support their assertion. Only One has risen, and multiple historical accounts attest to it.

Now, along with Sadhguru and Nithyananda, several other yogis and New Age people believe that they can become gods on their own and can be resurrected even if they die.

As I write, I'm reminded of a conversation with a skeptic who boldly declared, "I don't believe Jesus is God. I believe Jesus was an ordinary person who figured out how to unlock His supernatural capabilities and thus was able to do miracles like walking on water, healing people, etc. Which means we can also unlock those capabilities and have supernatural power like Him." He concluded saying, "One day people are going to learn how to unlock those capabilities, and you all are going to call them antichrist and persecute them." This gentleman believed he could be a superhero.

When I asked him about the resurrection of Jesus, he denied believing that Jesus was resurrected. In response, I asked him where he lived, to which he replied, "Atlanta." I then challenged his assertion, "I don't believe you live there." His reaction was telling—he seemed taken aback but ultimately shrugged it off with a casual "I don't care." This exchange illustrates a crucial point: he didn't feel the need to prove his residency because he knew he lived in Atlanta, and that was indeed a fact. Just as my disbelief in his residence didn't change the reality of where he lives, denial doesn't change the fact that Jesus is God and rose from the dead.

We can believe whatever we choose, but that doesn't change the truth. As humans, we need to acknowledge our lack of inherent supernatural power and our limitations. This is the first step in developing another important characteristic of a quality life: humility. Humility is "the feeling or attitude that you have no special importance that makes you better than others."[1]

The next step is acknowledging that only the living God possesses such power. We especially need the humility to build a relationship with God and cooperate with Him. We're going to look at how we can develop that in our own lives.

Humility to Build a Relationship with God

Our relationship with God is similar to that between parents and children. Good parents often understand what their children need even before the children ask for it. However, the children still express their desires to their parents, particularly on special occasions. Even though parents know what the children want, they wait for their children to ask. This dynamic fosters the development of the parent-child relationship and strengthens the bond between them.

Growing up, I observed many children who received everything from their parents even before they asked. Initially, it seemed like these children led a privileged life. However, over time, I noticed that the relationship between the children and their parents became transactional and demand-based, rather than personal and loving. The children began to feel entitled, expecting their parents to fulfill their every desire as a duty rather than appreciating what was provided. It was saddening.

On the other hand, when the children expressed their desires to their parents and the parents fulfilled them, it fostered a deeper connection between them. The children understood the importance of relying on their parents, and the parents demonstrated their unconditional love by meeting their children's needs and desires as they saw necessary. As a result, the parents and children still maintain a strong and affectionate relationship.

Similarly, although God is fully aware of our needs and desires, He expects us to ask Him for them so that He can fulfill them at the appropriate time. Imagine if God provided everything we needed and desired before we even asked Him, as He is fully capable of doing. In such a scenario, there would be no genuine relationship between us and God. We would fail to recognize our dependence on Him and our own limitations, and we would overlook the opportunity for God to demonstrate His unconditional love for us. As a result, instead of asking God for assistance and favors out of genuine need, we would come to expect them as entitlements. Therefore, God encourages us to freely ask Him for help and favors, and He is willing to fulfill them in His perfect timing.

Another aspect to consider is that sometimes God won't give us what we want, but He gives us what we need. When a child wants a particular toy or gadget that they see advertised or that their friends have, the child may passionately desire this item, believing it will bring them happiness and fulfillment. However, the parents, who have a broader perspective and understanding of their child's needs and priorities, may decide not to fulfill this specific request. Instead, they may choose to allocate resources towards family outings, educational materials, or extracurricular activities that they believe will contribute more significantly to their child's overall well-being and development.

In this example, the parents' decision reflects their deeper understanding of their child's needs and the broader context of their family life. Similarly, God, as a loving and omniscient parent, may withhold certain desires or grant different blessings in our lives, not out of a lack of care or concern, but because He sees the bigger picture and knows what will ultimately lead to quality of life.

These real-life scenarios illustrate the importance of humility in our relationship with God. First, acknowledging our lack of power and limitations will help us to develop humility. Second, we demonstrate humility when we humbly ask God for our needs and desires, recognizing that He is the ultimate provider. Third, humility is required to accept God's provisions and blessings, even if they differ from what we expected or desired. Finally, true humility is exemplified in our willingness to surrender to God's will completely, trusting that His plans are far greater than our own and fostering a healthy, intimate relationship with Him.

> *"Every good gift and every perfect gift is from above, and comes down from the Father of lights, with whom there is no variation or shadow of turning" (James 1:17).*

> *"If you then, being evil, know how to give good gifts to your children, how much more will your Father who is in heaven give good things to those who ask Him!" (Matthew 7:11)*

Humility to Cooperate with God

To understand why God expects us to cooperate with Him and how humility aids in this cooperation, let's look at a story from the first book of the Bible:

> *"When the morning dawned, the angels urged Lot to hurry, saying, 'Arise, take your wife and your two daughters who are here, lest you be consumed in the punishment of the city.' And while he lingered, the men*

> *took hold of his hand, his wife's hand, and the hands of his two daughters, the LORD being merciful to him, and they brought him out and set him outside the city. So it came to pass, when they had brought them outside, that he said, 'Escape for your life! Do not look behind you nor stay anywhere in the plain. Escape to the mountains, lest you be destroyed'" (Genesis 19:15–17).*

I would like you to notice something very important in this passage. Yes, God saved Lot and his family from the destruction of Sodom and Gomorrah. But have you ever wondered why God didn't simply instruct the angels to carry them away to the mountains? Why did the angels bring them only just outside the city and instruct them not to look back or stay nearby but to escape to the mountains?

It's not as though angels are incapable of carrying four humans, nor are they unable to fly, and they certainly wouldn't have become tired from escaping the city. So why didn't they just fly Job and his family away, as superheroes might? It would have potentially prevented Lot's wife from turning back to look at the city, which led to her transformation into a pillar of salt, as we see later in the chapter.

God never forces us to do His will but wants us to trust Him wholeheartedly and cooperate with Him in all our endeavors. Throughout the Bible, we can see that people worked alongside God to witness mighty miracles. For example, God gave the measurements and Noah built the ark *(Genesis 6:13–22)*; God directed and the Israelites walked out of Egypt from slavery *(Exodus 12:31–42)*; Elisha threw a stick in the water and God made the axe iron float *(2 Kings 6:1–7)*; Jesus multiplied the food and the disciples distributed it *(Mark 6:30–44)*. Working alongside God demonstrates faith, humility, and obedience, which are often necessary for the fulfillment of divine purposes.

In the case of Lot's wife, her pride and attachment to material things likely contributed to her downfall. Why do I say that? It says in *Ezekiel 16:49*,
> "Look, this was the iniquity of your sister Sodom: She and her daughter had pride, fullness of food, and abundance of idleness; neither did she strengthen the hand of the poor and needy."

Not just her, but all who lived in the land suffered from pride because they thought they had everything they needed, especially material things. This led them to idleness, which in turn led to committing abominations (wicked sins) before God (verse 50). If Lot's wife had humbled herself, she would have listened to what the angels had instructed and run to the mountains.

If Lot's wife prioritized obedience and cooperation with God's instructions, she might have been spared from the consequences of looking back and perishing. It's a powerful lesson about the dangers of pride and the importance of humility in following God's guidance.

Are there people who struggle with pride because of their wealth these days? Does that hinder them from having a genuine relationship with God? Don't get me wrong; having wealth doesn't necessarily mean you can't have a relationship with God, but many have shown that wealth significantly impacts their spiritual lives.

The issue isn't the wealth itself that steers people away from God but rather the pride that arises from wealth. Beyond wealth, anything that becomes an idol leading to pride can affect our connection with God. This could include accomplishments, job titles, professions, romantic relationships, education, or any source of pride.

My question to you is, Are you willing to give up everything for Jesus today? Is there anything that would hinder your relationship with God? Are you humble enough to cooperate with God in every situation? My challenge to you is to assess your willingness to surrender and cooperate with God unreservedly.

Many in this world boast of their achievements in raising their children, but in the process, they lose their spouses to someone else. Some claim success because they've amassed wealth, only to lose their families in the pursuit. Others boast of achievements while neglecting their health and going to a premature death.

While raising children, earning money, and gaining achievements are important aspects of life, doing them at the cost of other vital aspects is not true accomplishment. Those who recognize their limitations and set boundaries to prioritize their health, family, and relationships are the ones who truly succeed. Recognizing our limits, acknowledging God's omnipotence, and cooperating with Him will lead to the best quality of life.

Reflections:
1. What is the significance of acknowledging there is a God present in the universe?
2. What is the significance of recognizing that only God is omnipresent, omnipotent, and omniscient?

3. How would your life change if you acknowledged your limitations and recognized God's power?
4. Why is humility necessary to build your relationship with God?
5. In which areas of life do you believe you need to cooperate with God? List each one and consider why.

References
1. "Humility," *Cambridge Dictionary,* dictionary.cambridge.org.

QUALITY LIFE

Chapter Seven
VALUE
Did You Find Your Worth Yet?

——— ✦ ———

A person's value or self-worth plays a crucial role in shaping their identity, priorities, and sense of purpose, guiding them to make choices accordingly. Do you value who you are? Where do you find your value? Is it in your accomplishments, work, acceptance by others, popularity, external validation, physical health, financial wealth, IQ, awards, social media likes, or even relationships? Is there any other thing that you place your value in? Be honest with yourself and ponder this question.

When I was eight years old, I participated in a 100 meter running race organized by my local community in India. To my surprise, I came in first place. The following year, I competed again, and once more I came in first. But this time, my brother warned me that the guy who came in second was very close and that I needed to step up my game for the next year. This is a natural thought because the competitive world highly values first place. The moment you slip to second, it's easy to feel like your worth has diminished. When they award you the trophy for second place, you know it's not the same as first. Your ego may be hurt, even if you don't openly acknowledge it.

Here's a scenario on a grander scale. Someone that finishes first in an Olympic competition may find their value in that first place. The moment they come second, they feel their value is lowered, even though several others are behind them. Similarly, a businessperson who holds the number-one spot in the nation may base their value on their success. But the moment their competitor surpasses them, they may feel their worth has decreased, even though hundreds of others are below them.

In the entertainment industry, the value of movie stars and singers is determined by how successful their movies or songs are. The more hits they produce, the higher their pay and overall value become. Similarly, in sports, the team or individual's value increases when they win championships. This leads to higher pay, more sponsorships, and advertisement opportunities. However, if the same team or individual loses in the finals the following year, they may feel that their value has diminished, even if they made it to the finals. This is how the culture of competition has been ingrained in our society.

Likewise, churches and religions often find their value in the number of followers they have and their impact on their communities. When their congregation grows and their teachings resonate, they may feel their value is increasing. Yet, if they face controversies or a decline in membership, they might feel that their value has declined.

I could share many other scenarios, but I think you get the point. Individuals who achieve the top position in their respective fields often place a high value on that achievement, and they feel their value diminishes when they are surpassed by others, even if there are many others still behind them. This is the mindset we have built through generations. There is a competition or comparison in every single thing in life, whether spoken or unspoken.

Organized Competitions

I asked Chat GPT to list the top 20 competitions in the world, and below is the response I received:
1. *Olympic Games: The pinnacle of international sports competition.*
2. *FIFA World Cup: The most prestigious soccer (football) tournament.*
3. *Nobel Prizes: Recognizing outstanding contributions to humanity in various fields.*
4. *Academy Awards (Oscars): Honoring excellence in the film industry.*
5. *NBA Finals: The climax of the National Basketball Association season.*
6. *Super Bowl: The championship game of American football in the NFL.*
7. *Tour de France: The premier cycling race.*
8. *Wimbledon: One of the most prestigious tennis tournaments.*
9. *The Masters: A major golf tournament held at Augusta National Golf Club.*
10. *UEFA Champions League: The top European club soccer competition.*
11. *The World Chess Championship: A prestigious chess tournament.*
12. *America's Cup: A prestigious yacht racing competition.*
13. *Boston Marathon: One of the world's oldest and most prestigious marathons.*
14. *The Booker Prize: Recognizing outstanding fiction writing.*
15. *Grammy Awards: Celebrating achievements in the music industry.*
16. *Pulitzer Prizes: Recognizing excellence in journalism and literature.*

17. The Cannes Film Festival: A renowned film festival in France.
18. The Michelin Guide: Awarding stars to top restaurants and chefs.
19. The World Series of Poker: The largest and most prestigious poker tournament.
20. Google Code Jam: A prestigious coding competition for programmers.

How many of these competitions are you familiar with? These are just the top 20, so there are literally millions of other competitions worldwide, ranging from those within nations, states/provinces, cities, districts, schools, and beyond. Not to mention competition between businesses like Burger King, McDonald's, Domino's Pizza, and more. We have competitions for the physically and/or mentally challenged, such as the Paralympics, or competitions for babies who have no concept of what competition means. We've even brought animals into our competitive world.

But why do we have so many competitions? Is it merely to get first place by outdoing others? Of course, people often justify competition as healthy and essential for individual growth. They call them "healthy competitions." But is it truly healthy? Haven't we witnessed enough fights and quarrels during competitions? When we make others lose, we're only feeding our pride and ego, which, in turn, bolsters our self-worth. However, the moment we lose our higher position, that perceived value can vanish.

In India, we have competition introduced in the education system early on through the ranking system. This puts a lot of pressure on young people to perform well, not because they are interested in learning a particular subject but because of the family and social pressure. Many young individuals indeed face significant stress and anxiety due to societal expectations and pressures to meet certain social standards, which has led them to tragic outcomes such as suicide. Is this truly healthy competition?

Let's take a closer look at competition. First of all, what does the word competition or compete mean? The Britannica Dictionary gives the following definitions[1]:
1. "the act or process of trying to get or win something (such as a prize or a higher level of success) that someone else is also trying to get or win: the act or process of competing"
2. "actions that are done by people, companies, etc., that are competing against each other"
3. "the competition: a person or group that you are trying to succeed against: a person or group that you are competing with"
4. "a contest in which people try to win by being better, faster, etc., than others: an event in which people compete."

So, basically competition is the effort to achieve something, like a prize or success, that others are also trying to achieve. It can involve individuals, groups, or companies trying to outdo each other, often in contests where they aim to be better or faster than others. Even a war between countries can be seen as a form of competition. One country tries to succeed and achieve victory by conquering another country and establishing a new government system in the conquered territory.

Unspoken Competitions

Unspoken competitions refer to contests or rivalries that exist without explicit rules or announcements. These competitions are often informal and can involve individuals or groups vying for success or recognition without openly declaring their intentions. These competitions may be based on social, personal, or professional goals and can be subtle, with participants competing for various achievements without openly acknowledging it.

Examples of unspoken competitions are:
- **Office politics:** In your workplace, you may silently compete with your coworkers for promotions, recognition, or the boss's favor.
- **Social media:** On social media platforms, you may compete for the most likes, comments, or followers. You post carefully curated content to project a certain image or lifestyle, trying to outdo your friends or peers without explicitly stating it.
- **Parenting:** You compete with other parents in various ways, such as who has the most well-behaved children, who attends the most extracurricular activities, or who throws the best birthday parties.
- **Dating and relationships:** In the dating world, you may compete for the attention and affection of someone you are interested in. This competition can manifest in subtle ways, like trying to be more interesting or attractive than others in the dating pool.
- **Academic achievement:** In schools and universities, you may aim to get the highest grades and outperform your classmates.
- **Sportsmanship:** You may compete among your team members for playing time or recognition from coaches. You push yourself harder during practice and games to prove your worth, fostering a competitive spirit even without explicitly discussing your rivalry.

- **Fashion and style:** You may try to outdo others in terms of your makeup, clothing choices or brands, accessories, or overall appearance to establish yourselves as a trendsetter or fashion influencer or even just to feel better than others.
- **Neighborhood and homeownership:** In your neighborhood, you might compete to have the most well-maintained property or the most attractive landscaping.
- **Charity and philanthropy:** You may be part of a wealthy community or organization, where people engage in unspoken competition to make the largest charitable donations or sponsor the highest profile charitable events so that they enhance their public image and reputation.
- **Fitness and health:** You may try to surpass your friends or acquaintances by having a bigger physique or lifting heavier weights or doing the highest reps.
- **Physical appearance:** You may often compare your physical appearance with that of others, whether friends, celebrities, or peers. You wish to be considered more attractive than those you admire or envy.
- **Husband and wife:** You may have competition about financial success, parenting styles, household chores (especially who does more than the other), initiating intimacy, personal achievements, control, decision-making, appearance, and expressing love for each other.
- **Sibling rivalry:** This rivalry may be vocalized when you are young and competing over who has the better height, attention from others, grades, and friends. However, as you grow up, it can become an unspoken competition as you compare yourself with your siblings in terms of financial status, partner, children, retirement benefits, house, vacations, or physical condition.

These examples illustrate that unspoken competition can manifest in various aspects of life, often driven by a desire for recognition, status, or personal satisfaction. It's important to recognize these dynamics. Do you relate with any of these examples?

Competition, both spoken and unspoken, has existed throughout the history of life on Earth. Yet, the question remains: when and where did the concept of competition originate? While the earliest recorded competitions can be traced back to the ancient civilizations of Greece and Rome, the idea of competing and outdoing others likely didn't start with sports alone. Competition has manifested in various forms throughout history, including nations competing against one another in wars long before organized sports emerged. So, when exactly did competition originate?

The Origin of Competition

Isaiah 14:13–14 reveals the thoughts the angel Lucifer had in heaven: *"For you have said in your heart: ... I will exalt my throne above the stars of God ... I will be like the Most High."* Lucifer used to be the *"anointed cherub" (Ezekiel 28:14)* in heaven who later rebelled against God and became Satan. In this story, we witness the first-ever instances of discontent, competition, and identity crisis recorded in the entire universe. Lucifer, in his jealousy, sought to surpass his own Creator. He failed to recognize the value bestowed upon him by his Creator and attempted to gain value by rebelling against the Most High, convincing other angels to join his cause. Consequently, *"war broke out in heaven"* (Revelation 12:7).

When Satan and his angels were unable to *"prevail, nor was a place found for them in heaven any longer" (Revelation 12:8)*, he, along with *"a third of the stars"* or angels, was *"cast to the earth" (Revelation 12:4, 9)*. Even after being cast down to Earth from heaven, Satan remained unrepentant, continuing to harbor feelings of discontent, jealousy, and self-centeredness. These negative traits caused him to disregard his own inherent value.

Bringing these attributes with him into our world, he insidiously introduced them into the minds of humanity, starting with Eve. Consequently, he introduced both spoken and unspoken competition into our world, deceiving people into not seeing where their value lies. This deception led people to become discontented, jealous, and self-centered. They began to seek their value by competing with and surpassing others.

The Bible on Competition

In contrast to Satan's negative traits of discontentment, jealousy, and self-centeredness, the Bible teaches us to be content and selfless, esteeming others better than ourselves. Nowhere in the Bible do we see God promoting competition. In fact, God repeatedly commands us to live in peace and harmony with one another. Even when we look at the context of the wars in the Bible, all the wars God allowed His children to fight served a different purpose than wars driven by greed, power, and personal gain. The wars in the Bible were often fought to protect God's people or carry out His divine plan.

During a conversation with His disciples, Jesus addressed the concept of competition. When they inquired, *"Who then is the greatest in the kingdom of heaven?" (Matthew 18:1)* Jesus replied, *"Assuredly, I say to you, unless you are converted and become as little children, you will by no means enter the kingdom of heaven. Therefore, whoever humbles himself as this little child is the greatest in the kingdom of heaven"* (Matthew 18:3–4).

I want to emphasize that Jesus didn't suggest that whoever gave the most Bible studies or baptized the most people would be the greatest in the kingdom of heaven. His response also indicates that there can be multiple "greatest" individuals in the kingdom of heaven. In other words, Jesus didn't promote competition. Instead, anyone can be the greatest in His kingdom, as long as they embrace humility and let go of their competitive nature.

Several references in the Bible show that God doesn't approve of competition:

> *"Pride goes before destruction, and a haughty spirit before a fall"* (Proverbs 16:18).

> *"Again, I saw that for all toil and every skillful work a man is envied by his neighbor. This also is vanity and grasping for the wind"* (Ecclesiastes 4:4).

> *"Let nothing be done through selfish ambition or conceit, but in lowliness of mind let each esteem others better than himself"* (Philippians 2:3).

> *"But if you have bitter envy and self-seeking in your hearts, do not boast and lie against the truth. This wisdom does not descend from above, but is earthly, sensual, demonic. For where envy and self-seeking exist, confusion and every evil thing are there"* (James 3:14–16).

Finding Value in Competition

So far, we've explored various types of competition, its origins, and how it's viewed in the Bible. But how does competition affect our value? As we've seen, competition or comparison is present in all aspects of our lives, and it shapes our perception of our value. When we outperform others, we feel more valuable, and when we don't, we feel less valuable. Unfortunately, this mindset is ingrained in us from a young age, leading us to believe that our worth is determined by how we compare to others.

Sometimes, we might not even intentionally realize it, but we end up competing with others because of this mindset Satan instilled in society. For example, I recently came across an Instagram post stating that an eleven-year-old girl with autism has a higher IQ than Albert Einstein and Stephen Hawking. Do you see anything wrong with this news? I do!

We can appreciate Adhara Pérez Sánchez's incredible IQ of 162. But while comparing her to Einstein and Hawking may seem to provide a perspective of her intelligence, it still conveys a sense of competition, similar to how someone being more muscular than Arnold Schwarzenegger at his peak would be viewed.
The writers of the post could have just stated that an eleven-year-old girl with autism has an IQ of 162—which is classified under the "Exceptional" category2—and is soon receiving her master's degree in engineering. They could have elaborated on her accomplishments and ambitions, which would have provided sufficient evidence to reveal her intelligence.

Through the wording in the news, we see evidence of Satan's subtle device of destruction. Outwardly, it doesn't seem like a big issue because it has become a common practice in daily life, but it will when it hits home. If your children constantly lose to their peers in competitions, can you imagine the damage it will wreak in their hearts? Can you imagine how their self-value will be diminished?

The same deception that ensnared Satan himself is a pitfall we can also fall into. If you feel you can find your value solely from outdoing others, you tread on a dangerous path. While seeking external validation is natural in this sinful world, relying solely on it is problematic because it's ever-changing. The more you base your self-worth on outperforming others, the more you feed your ego. This unhealthy competition can lead to intemperance in various aspects of life, whether it's in the pursuit of wealth, extravagant spending, or a relentless drive to be the best in sports or any other area that resonates with your daily life.

It's important for us to recognize the harmful effects of competition and work towards building a culture of collaboration and encouragement. We are not built to compete but to support and strengthen each other. How many of you have seen videos in which one person supports another person right in the middle of an intense race? When that happens, no matter who wins that race, people are more glued to the support and kindness that is displayed. In that very moment, everything slows down, our inner kindness is awakened, and as we witness that delightful sight, we start cheering for the two to cross the finish line. We might even forget the person who won the race, but we'll never forget that act of kindness for the rest of our lives.

Instead of competing against each other, we should focus on identifying and nurturing our unique strengths and abilities. We should celebrate each other's successes and support each other's growth. By doing so, we can create a world where everyone can thrive and reach their full potential without feeling the need to compete or compare themselves to others. Let's break free from the chains of the competitive mindset and embrace a more compassionate and inclusive way of living.

Value in Overwork

When people find their value in work, it can become an addiction. Addiction is a continuously intensifying problem if not addressed. In this situation, it results in overwork. They obsess over their work so much that they feel restless when they are not working. This obsession can lead to rumination about work and even insomnia.

When these individuals aren't working, even while on vacation, they may feel like their value is diminished. The suffering they experience as a result reveals their underlying insecurity. The more they work, the more they believe they have value. This intemperate mindset breaks all the boundaries, negatively impacting health, relationships, and overall quality of life.

Value in Ministry

For some Christians, serving in ministry—whether volunteering at church, working for an organization, or running their own—brings a sense of purpose and fulfillment. Being appreciated and praised for their contributions is a source of validation and satisfaction. Such individuals might be willing to sacrifice their money, health, personal time, and family time in the name of ministry.

Valuing oneself primarily through ministry sacrifices and achievements can create a performance-based mindset. This means, even though most might not verbalize it, they expect to be appreciated or praised for their sacrifices and hard work.

If they are not recognized, their sense of value takes a hit. In turn, they work more and more, leading to burnout, bitterness, resentment, backbiting, neglect of important relationships, and spiritual crisis.

I have witnessed some individuals, when not recognized for their ministerial work, experiencing identity crises, becoming less active in ministry, and even leaving their faith. They blamed God, reasoning that despite their hard work for Him, He didn't recognize their efforts. Thus, it's crucial to avoid linking one's value and self-worth to ministry.

Value in Romantic Relationships

Millions find value in social media likes and comments, while others find it at school, work, the salon, or clothing stores. Yet others find their value from their romantic partner.

But the moment we place our worth on others' opinions and feelings, we are submitting ourselves to them. While we may enjoy compliments, we can't make those the measure of our value, even when they come from romantic partners. Why do I say that? The same people that compliment you can be the people that tear you down.

Some couples experience a rude awakening when they realize their partner's love is driven purely by feelings and emotions.

When these feelings and emotions fade, the validation from their partner diminishes. In many cases, they begin to talk negatively about their partner, including the very traits they once appreciated.

You might argue that not everyone has a relationship driven solely by emotions and that your relationship or marriage is more mature, rooted in true love. You might wonder why it isn't okay to find value in the words and actions of your romantic partner.

While it's natural to appreciate your partner's affirmation, if you depend solely on them to find your value, you risk lowering or losing your sense of self-worth when they don't consistently uphold their actions or words. In these situations, you might become willing to compromise your temperance and boundaries, resulting in clinginess and stress within the relationship, all in the hope that they will give you the attention they once did. This isn't healthy and can be a symptom of anxious attachment.

Our self-worth should never be reliant on external validation. Otherwise, we can end up in a toxic cycle of seeking validation and feeling inadequate when we don't receive it.

Instead, we should focus on building a strong sense of self-worth and confidence, independent of others' opinions.

Being Like God

When and how did we learn to seek our value and self-worth in external factors? It all started at the very creation of humanity while the earth was still young. Satan made Eve question her self-worth, suggesting that she needed to become someone else to gain value and experience true confidence. Satan planted the idea that who she was in her natural state wasn't enough, deceiving her by saying that she could be "like God."

Satan could have said she would become wiser than she was, or that she would better comprehend things than her husband. He could have suggested she could be like angels or even the leader of the angelic host. But he didn't. Instead, he made the emphatic statement, *"You will be like God" (Genesis 3:5)*. This stemmed from his own desire to be like God. He had roamed the universe in search of ways to achieve this. Perhaps he had even tried different methods. Regardless, we can infer that he ensnared Eve in the same deception that had ensnared him: *"You will be like God."*

Since Eve's time, he has been deceiving billions, if not trillions, of people in this world with the same deceptive phrase, *"You will be like God."* Even before Eve, he had deceived one-third of the angels. If he has been doing that for millennia, he will try to deceive you and me with the same ideology.

Satan knows that if he can make us feel discontent with who we are and lure us into constantly striving to show who we can become, then our sense of value becomes easily shaken. By sowing seeds of dissatisfaction and encouraging us to chase an idealized version of ourselves, he undermines our inherent worth and stability. This strategy introduces comparison, jealousy, and self-centeredness into our lives.

Though we may not outright believe that we will be like gods in our pursuit of being the best, we still develop intemperate mindsets. These include desires to control others, to have complete authority over our lives, to adopt extreme lifestyle practices in the hope of living forever, to perform good deeds solely to receive good in return, and to believe that being fallible is inherently wrong. These mindsets ultimately lead us away from a healthy sense of self and towards a constant state of dissatisfaction and unrest.

Do not fall for these mindsets. Someone who has been created can never truly be like God. This idea originated from a discontent and self-centered hearts. Traits that are unique to God, often referred to as His "incommunicable attributes," set Him apart from all other beings in this universe and make it impossible for us to become like Him. These attributes include:

- **Omnipotence (being all-powerful):** God's ability to do anything that is logically possible and doesn't go against His perfect character. He has unlimited power and authority over all creation *(Luke 1:37)*. Only God can create, sustain, and govern the universe with absolute power. Human beings, in contrast, are limited in power and capability.
- **Omniscience (being all-knowing):** God's complete and perfect knowledge of all things past, present, and future. He understands everything fully and instantly *(Psalm 147:5)*. Unlike humans who learn and discover, God knows all things inherently and eternally. Nothing is hidden from Him.
- **Omnipresence (being present everywhere):** God's ability to be present in all places at all times. He transcends spatial limitations and is fully present everywhere *(Psalm 139:7)*. Humans and other beings are confined to one place at a time, but God is simultaneously present everywhere.
- **Aseity (self-existence and independence):** God's existence

is not dependent on anything outside of Himself. He is self-sufficient and the source of all existence *(Exodus 3:14)*. While all other beings rely on something for their existence, God is the uncaused cause who exists by necessity of His own nature.

- **Immutability (unchanging nature)**: God's nature, character, and will are constant and unchangeable. He is the same yesterday, today, and forever *(Malachi 3:6)*. Human beings and all creation are subject to change, growth, and decay, but God remains perfectly consistent and reliable.
- **Eternality (timeless existence)**: God exists outside of time and has no beginning or end *(Psalm 90:2)*. Humans and other beings are bound by the flow of time, with a beginning and an end, but God exists eternally beyond time.
- **Simplicity (unity and indivisibility)**: God is not composed of parts; His attributes and essence are unified and indistinguishable from His being. Every attribute of God is God *(Deuteronomy 6:4)*. Human beings have composite natures with different parts and qualities, but God is completely unified and cannot be divided.
- **Sovereignty (supreme authority)**: God rules over all creation. He orchestrates everything according to His divine will and purpose *(Psalm 103:19)*. Human authority is limited and derived, but God's sovereignty is absolute and independent of any external force.

No human or being in this universe can become like God. Divinity is not a status one can achieve; it is an intrinsic attribute of a being who alone deserves true worship. The pursuit of becoming like God, which Satan subtly tempts us to join, is a futile and dangerous endeavor. It distracts us from accepting and embracing our true worth as created beings, leading us instead down a path of perpetual dissatisfaction and unending comparison.

Value and Temperance

To understand the connection between value and temperance, we need to first understand what temperance is. Merriam-Webster defines it as "moderation in action, thought and feeling"3—a common way of understanding it. But, in reality, this definition isn't true!

Why do I say that? Temperance isn't just about controlling our cravings or desires but also about recognizing which choices are healthy and which are harmful. It's about understanding moderation and abstinence. It's about making choices that are good for us and avoiding those that are not.

For example, can someone with stage 4 cancer be temperate by choosing to eat just one slice of cake instead of two? Knowing that cancer feeds on sugar, the person must completely avoid eating cake. Or would you allow your child to drink in moderation? No! You wouldn't allow them to drink at all because you know how it would harm them.

In practicing temperance, we choose good things in moderation, such as enjoying delicious food, staying hydrated, studying for exams, engaging in physical exercise, spending time on screens, and even being intimate with our partner. On the other hand, some things are better abstained from, such as intoxication, frequent late-night parties, unnecessary debt, toxic relationships, and gambling. To sum it up, temperance involves avoiding negative influences and partaking in positive ones in moderation.

Temperance allows us to make informed decisions for a

balanced and fulfilling life. It's about taking care of ourselves so that we can have a quality life.

So, how is value related to temperance? When someone seeks to derive personal value or worth from something, they tend to lose self-control and become intemperate, thus losing their identity. This pattern has persisted since Lucifer was in heaven and has continued for millennia. It can manifest in various ways, such as becoming addicted to substances or behaviors, obsessing over success or recognition, or experiencing low self-esteem and self-worth. It leaves people feeling discouraged and hopeless. As we try to find or maintain value in other things, we inadvertently encourage an intemperate mindset.

Where Does Your Value Come From Anyway?

We all possess inherent value, bestowed upon us by our Creator, and it's our responsibility to acknowledge it. This intrinsic value is unalterable and can't be added to or taken away from us. It's natural to think that you could do something to add more value to yourself. Although it may seem like a great thought, there is a problem there. The moment you think you can add more value to yourself, you open the door to losing your value as well. Then, we fall into the same rut we've been running into all these years—trying to add more value to ourselves and competing with others to have more value than them. These efforts will lead to becoming intemperate and, in turn, losing our quality of life.

Satan lost sight of his inherent value and began comparing himself to his Creator, ultimately leading him to rebel. This rebellion led to a host of negative attributes, including intemperance. Satan managed to deceive one-third of the angels and has since been responsible for deceiving trillions of people, including both you and me. Even now, if Satan were to recognize his inherent value given by his Creator and repent of his ways, God would accept him into His kingdom. But unfortunately, Satan won't change his ways.

A Silver Coin

"Or what woman, having ten silver coins, if she loses one coin, does not light a lamp, sweep the house, and search carefully until she finds it? And when she has found it, she calls her friends and neighbors together, saying, *'Rejoice with me, for I have found the piece which I lost!'" (Luke 15:8–9)*

The interpretation of this parable is that God goes in search of lost sinners and rejoices over even one repentant sinner. But why did Jesus use silver coins in this parable? Could it be because of the high value He has placed on His children? Jesus explains that the woman lights a lamp, sweeps the house, and searches every bit of her house until she finds the coin. But why does she have to search for it? Because of its high value.

If what she lost was of little value, say a piece of gravel, she wouldn't bother to search for it and rejoice with others. Even if it's in the dark, the silver coin is of high value. It doesn't lose its value even if it's covered in dust. The silver coin is of high value even when it's lost. The value is inherent, and it doesn't change in any circumstance. So it is with us! Our Jesus has placed on us a high value. We don't lose our value in any circumstance.

Though we may be in the dust, though we may become poor, though we may end up sick, though we may have an accident and lose part of our body, though we may lose our beauty, though we may fail in our classes, though we may be ridiculed, though we may be divorced, though we may be single for most of our life, though we may be slow to learn, though we may feel guilty because of our past, we can still believe we are of high value because we know who has given that value to us. We just have to humbly accept it.

Rather than being easily shaken, we can build our foundation on the Rock, Jesus *(1 Corinthians 10:4; Matthew 16:18)*. We don't need people or things to give us value. Of course, this doesn't mean being prideful of who we are. But having our value in Christ will give us constant assurance of our great value. It will keep us from falling into the snares Satan has laid out for us. We'll feel content with who we are and what we have.

Diamond Ring

While I was training to be a flight attendant, my instructor shared a story with us about the need for flight attendants to be willing to serve. I'll never forget the story. During one of the flights, a lady lost her ring in the toilet bowl. After the flight landed, a crew member put on five sets of gloves and tried to find the diamond ring among the sewage. After a long search, they succeeded and returned the diamond ring back to its owner. We were all disgusted but amazed at how they found the ring.

This story also teaches another lesson. Even if a diamond ring falls into the sewer, it's still a diamond ring. The value of it doesn't change or diminish. If someone else finds it, they wouldn't say, "Ew, yuck!" If they knew the value of it, they would definitely take it, wash it, and use it for their good.

VALUE

When Satan tempted Eve in *Genesis 3:1–6*, Satan was cunning. He made her question her value and her contentment as God's child. He made her wonder if she could be better than she was and have more than she had. We could summarize Satan's temptation like this:
1. Satan lied.
2. He made God look like a liar.
3. He convinced Eve that she would become wiser than she was.
4. He told her that she wasn't enough, even in her perfect unfallen state.
5. He told her that she could be like God and have greater value.

Compare these temptations to your life and see if Satan has tempted and deceived you the same way he did Eve:
1. Does he say that you should do more to please God? Does he say that you should do more to please others? Does he lie to you about your identity?
2. Do you sometimes believe that God is the one who has brought so much suffering into your life or your loved one's life? Does Satan make you believe that God is withholding the things that will make you a better person or give you a better life?
3. Do you believe that you can be a superhero or that God might have given you a secret power you haven't recognized yet? Have you been influenced by Marvel movies, Disney movies, or DC movies? Do you believe you're smarter than others? Do you believe others are smarter than you?
4. Does Satan tempt you to believe you need to prove to yourself and others that you are "someone"? Does Satan

make you feel like you accomplish something when you say you identify yourself as someone or something else? Do you feel a sense of value when you go on Pride rallies with your partners or friends? If you truly are perfect the way you are, then why do you feel the need to change your gender or identity?
5. Do you feel you can be like God? How many times have you called yourself and others a god or goddess? Do you feel like you are missing out on something that would make you better than others and maybe even God?

These are some questions for you to ponder. If you can relate to any of them, then know that the devil, that old serpent, is deceiving you as he did Eve and putting the blame on God. Remember, God has given you great value just as you are. You can live in His peace. But Satan wants you to ignore your existing value so that you'll suffer and be discontent throughout your life.

When Jesus said that the path to heaven is narrow, He meant it. The moment we go outside of the safety zone Jesus has given us, we fall into the devil's deception. Satan either wants you to believe that you are worthless or that you are of more worth than others because you are "divine."

It's not about being divine but rather acknowledging the immense worth bestowed upon us by the Creator. By accepting this value, you can avoid many heartaches and become content. Contentment, in turn, will lead to temperance in everything—avoiding what is bad and taking the good in moderation. So, let's strive for temperance in all that we do and make choices that are good for our minds, bodies, and souls. Doing so is another step toward a quality life.

Reflection:
1. Take a moment to think about where you find your value.
2. Organize your life in decades and think about the highlight of each decade. That will help you recognize where you have placed your value in each decade.
3. Why do you want to change certain things in your life? Is doing so a want or a need?
4. What motivates you to change who you are?
5. How would your life be different if you knew your value is in your Creator and not in what you do? Your value cannot change.

References
1. *"Competition," The Britannica Dictionary,* britannica.com/dictionary.
2. *"IQ Tests," IQ Test Foundation,* iqtestfoundation.org/en/iq-tests.
3. *"Temperance," Merriam-Webster,* merriam-webster.com.

Chapter Eight
FAITH
Something We All Possess

Faith is a term that embodies complete trust or belief in someone or something, often oriented towards a hopeful or positive outcome. In our day-to-day lives, we all exercise faith in various people or things. We're never entirely self-reliant.

In this chapter, we'll explore the profound connection between faith and eternal life. But why focus on eternal life, you might ask? Living forever is commonly regarded as the highest and most desirable outcome that one could hope to achieve through faith, regardless of religious or belief orientation.

Around the world, many people, whether theists—such as Christians, Muslims, and Hindus—or atheists—such as Ray Kurzweil, Aubrey de Grey, and historical figures like Qin Shi Huang—yearn to live forever. Their pursuit of eternal life is guided by their respective understandings of how it might be attained.

For most theists, eternal life is a reward granted by their deities for living in accordance with the divine will. Conversely, many atheists turn to science and technology, exploring avenues like cryonics, genetic engineering, or artificial intelligence as the means to achieve immortality.

People prefer to achieve eternal life through their own strength, believing that this self-reliance provides them with a sense of control and assurance—similar to how people depend on money to secure food, shelter, and other basic needs. However, attaining eternal life through faith in an unseen God requires a different approach, where faith plays a pivotal role.

As we go through this chapter, we'll discuss how people question and debate about the existence of God, and different beliefs people have about gaining eternal life. Then, we'll look at God's desire to grant us eternal life and the role of faith in this process.

Questioning the Existence of God

Throughout history, people have been drawn to complex explanations for the origin of life. Various theories and belief systems have been developed in attempts to prove that we evolved over millions, if not billions, of years. Yet, the mystery of how everything came into being remains unsolved. We still don't have answers to questions about what happened before the Big Bang Theory or how atoms and nuclei came into existence.

Many people believe that science can provide answers to the mysteries of life and the universe. However, despite advances in scientific knowledge and technology, there are still many unanswered questions about the origins of the universe and life itself. The pursuit of knowledge and understanding in this area continues.

"People seem to always prefer the complicated way when it comes to life and the universe—whether it's about the infinite past or the endless future."

People seem to always prefer the complicated way when it comes to life and the universe—whether it's about the infinite past or the endless future. Perhaps it's because we are curious beings and we're always exploring and understanding the universe around us.

Could it be that the mysteries of the universe and the complexities of life fascinate us and compel us to unravel their secrets because we want fame for ourselves? Could this quest for knowledge lead us down convoluted paths, obscuring the simple truths that lie right in front of us? Let's explore further.

During many nights of my childhood, I often found myself in tears, struggling to comprehend the vastness of the universe. My young mind was unable to grasp its magnitude. Later, I realized that even grown adults couldn't answer those questions from an evolutionary standpoint.

What lies far beyond the sky? Where can we find the ends of the universe? Is there even an end of the universe? If we find the ends, what lies beyond them? Who created what lies beyond? What kind of beings live there? How long has the universe existed? How long will it endure into the future? These were questions I pondered.

No one has ever been able to provide definitive answers to these questions because no one has ever traveled far enough from Earth compared to the vastness of the universe, nor has anyone lived long enough compared to the existence of Earth and the universe itself.

Is it safe to say that all the *"answers"* we currently have are just speculations about what could be? I don't blame people for speculating because they're trying their best to make sense of what they can comprehend on their own. But nonetheless, we're still on a quest to find out the real answer.

Could it be that we overlook the simple solutions right in front of us? We may be guilty of overcomplicating things, searching for answers that meet our expectations of complexity. Despite all the progress we've made in the past century, what if we've missed the fact that the answers we seek have been available to us all along? Perhaps we don't even need the advancements in science to find them. We may need to adjust our perspective and look at things with a fresh set of eyes.

When it comes to questioning evolution, we can make some simple observations. For instance, why don't we see things naturally coming together or evolving before our very eyes? Another question that often arises is whether we all descended from a single monkey or from several different ones. If the latter is the case, shouldn't we see monkeys evolving into humans even now? And aside from monkeys, shouldn't we see other animals, trees, or plants evolving into entirely new species? We don't have any record of macroevolution in the last six thousand years.

Wouldn't it be easy to believe in a God who has existed from eternity past and will continue to exist into the future? Wouldn't it be easier to believe that He brought various entities, including us, into existence? Wouldn't it be easier to comprehend that there is a higher power in control of everything, rather than feeling alone and adrift in a vast and uncertain universe?

Believing in God is not a guarantee that all the questions we have will be answered, at least for now. In fact, it often leads to even more questions. For instance, some may ask who created God, how long God has been in existence, and whether God will live forever. Others may wonder how long time has been in existence and how long we will live in heaven. These are all valid questions that we may not have straightforward answers to right now, but they can certainly lead to deeper reflections and contemplations about the nature of God and the mysteries of life.

The Drive Behind Debating God's Existence

People often have a strong drive or passion to debate on various topics. What are the underlying reasons behind debates between Christians and atheists?

I've often encountered debates between theists and atheists aimed at discussing and concluding whether there is a God or not. These debates are focused on persuading one another to accept their respective beliefs as correct. Both arguments can sound very convincing. However, in such debates, a definitive conclusion is often elusive. This could be due to the absence of compelling evidence or because participants are more intent on asserting their own beliefs rather than being open to persuasion.

It always intrigues me to witness these debates because, as someone who believes in God, I find value in challenging myself with the questions posed by atheists. However, I recently had an aha moment. While pondering these debates on the existence of God, I realized that a Christian doesn't just engage in debate for the sake of debate. Christians often have a deeper reason for debate: to follow the Great Commission Jesus gave to His followers to share the truth.

This commission entails spreading His teachings, preaching the gospel, and making disciples throughout the world by baptizing them in the name of the Father, the Son, and the Holy Spirit. Additionally, Jesus urged His disciples to serve as witnesses of His message to the ends of the earth *(Matthew 28:19, 20; Mark 16:15; Luke 24:46–49; John 20:21; Acts 1:8).*

As Christians, we are recipients of the profound forgiveness, love, and grace demonstrated by Jesus. It's not just a duty but a joyful obligation to share these blessings with others. How can we withhold such transformative gifts, especially when we are aware of the promise of a heavenly kingdom?

When God takes His followers to that kingdom, He *"will wipe away every tear from their eyes; there shall be no more death, nor sorrow, nor crying. There shall be no more pain, for the former things have passed away.' Then He who sat on the throne said, 'Behold, I make all things new'" (Revelation 21:4–5).* This promise serves as our motivation to spread the message of redemption and hope to all.

With this understanding, it only makes sense that Christians are eager to spread the gospel and help people see the real love of Jesus. This doesn't mean that there aren't people that use the gospel message to exploit people and make money, and it also doesn't mean that there aren't Christians who force people to believe in Jesus and threaten them with hellfire. Both are wrong ways to spread the gospel. All Christians are given a balanced responsibility to spread the gospel and share how one could have a quality life now and forever by accepting Jesus in their lives.

Now, what about those who don't believe in God? If there is no God and hence no rewards or repercussions, then what is the purpose of engaging in a debate to convince others that there is no God? Why do people debate when they do not believe in a higher power? If there is no God and no concept of an afterlife or eternal life, then what is the significance of such debates?

I do recognize that some individuals enjoy participating in debates as a means to explore ideas, challenge their own beliefs, and interact with diverse viewpoints. Debating the existence of God can be intellectually stimulating, irrespective of personal beliefs. However, attempting to use a debate to persuade others to adopt one's perspective seems futile. Whether someone lives as a believer in a god should not matter for the non-believer because all will pass away with their knowledge, which will ultimately have no impact on those around them.

If there is no God or afterlife, and I pass away, I won't be impacted; I will simply return to dust. If I hold the belief system of an atheist, there will be no change in the earth or even in the universe. However, if there is a God, and throughout my life, I have been convincing others to reject the idea of God, only to discover after my death that God does exist, what then? It would be a sorrowful awakening, a realization that arrives too late. So, it would make sense, then, to at least carefully weigh the evidence for God.

Evidence for a Creator

If you were ignorant about the true God all your life and then passed away, would He give you a second chance at life with a knowledge of Him? It seems only fair to expect God, especially a God of love, to grant us a second chance due to our ignorance.

However, we should remember that throughout this life, God

has already given us endless evidence and second chances to learn about Him. He has specifically shed light on His true identity in at least three different ways: through His words (the Bible), through His creation (nature), and through personal experiences with Him:

God's Word

The Bible states, *"All Scripture is given by inspiration of God" (2 Timothy 3:16)*, suggesting that the Holy Bible itself is a divine revelation. These Scriptures offers numerous insights into the existence of a Creator, particularly through two aspects: historical events and fulfilled prophecies.

> *"The historical events recorded in the Scriptures align closely with those found in non-religious history books, and in some instances, these biblical accounts have been used to guide archaeological discoveries."*

Below is some evidence for it:

> "Much of the Bible, in particular the historical books of the Old Testament, are as accurate historical documents as any that we have from antiquity and are in fact more accurate than many of the Egyptian, Mesopotamian, or Greek histories. These Biblical records can be and are used as are other ancient documents in archeological work. For the most part, historical events described took place and the peoples cited really existed. This is not to say that names of all peoples and places mentioned can be identified today, or that every event as reported in the historical books happened exactly as stated."[1]

One Israeli archeologist wrote: "What is amazing about the Bible is that very often we see that it is very accurate and sometimes amazingly accurate."[2]

Many prophecies in the Bible were fulfilled. Here is just one instance:

> "Fulfilled Bible prophecy is one way the Bible authenticates itself and shows us its reliability. ... Nebuchadnezzar's dream prophesied four successive world empires that would be followed by a divided kingdom, and each one of those has come true in history—from Babylon to the multitude of European countries."[3]

God's Creation

While closely related to the previous point, this angle emphasizes the direct evidence of a Creator visible in the natural world. Many people spend their lives exploring and studying the origins and mysteries of the universe, seeking to understand the intricacies of existence. The Holy Bible, however, offers profound insights into these questions, presenting answers provided by the Creator Himself.

The Bible covers the origins of all creation: the earth and sky, the sun, moon, and stars, the drifting clouds, and the vast oceans. It explains the existence of trees, animals, and deep canyons, as well as the diversity of languages, the changing seasons, and the cycles of planting and harvesting. Most importantly, it speaks of us humans, our purpose, and our connection to everything found in nature.

Through its descriptions and teachings, the Bible reveals a Creator who is personally involved in every aspect of the natural world through its intricate design and meticulous orchestration.

Each element, from the grandest galaxy to the smallest seed, is a testament to the deliberate and thoughtful design of the Creator. This connection between the scriptural accounts and the observable world serves as a compelling evidence of a divine hand in the origins and continuing existence of the universe.

Personal Experiences with God

Along with all this evidence, countless individuals have experienced God's mercy, grace, and love firsthand, becoming living witnesses to others. Their lives are transformed in ways that speak volumes about the presence and power of the Creator. One such example involves a person who had a profound encounter with God, a story my grandfather shared with my brother and me from his own youth.

Born into a life of privilege in Patiala State, North India, in 1889, Sundar Singh was the son of a wealthy Sikh landowner. Though he was born into a Hindu family and was taught by a sadhu—an ascetic Hindu holy man—who lived in a remote forest, his mother later sent him to a Christian school in hopes he'd have the best education.

In this Christian school led by missionaries, he learned English but was also introduced to Christianity. When Singh was 14 years old, his mother suddenly died, leaving him devastated and upset with religion.

One night when he was determined to commit suicide on a railway track, he had a lifechanging encounter with the Creator. He said, "Jesus came into my room. As I was praying for the last time a bright cloud of light suddenly filled the room … and out of the brightness came the face and figure of Jesus. He spoke to me. … 'How long will you persecute Me? I have come to save you. You were praying to know the right way; why do you not take it? I am the Way.' He spoke in Hindustani, and He spoke to me."[4]

While Sundar Singh's death remains a mystery, he lived a life testifying to others the presence of a true Creator—Jesus Christ.

It just makes perfect sense when we observe the world around us—historical events, fulfilled prophecies, nature, and personal experiences—all aligning with what we learn, see, and experience. Have you had an encounter with Jesus yet? If not, I strongly recommend you have an encounter with Him for a life-changing experience.

Different Beliefs on Gaining Eternal Life

So far, we have discussed how attempting to persuade others to believe in the absence of a god is futile. We have also explored the various aspects and tangible evidence on Earth that point to the existence of a living God. And if there is a God, then there is the possibility of eternal life.

But what is eternal life? Different individuals perceive it in different ways. As we discussed earlier in this chapter, there is a group that doesn't believe in a god and, consequently, doesn't believe in any form of life beyond this one. Hence, we won't discuss more about this viewpoint. But when it comes to belief in God and eternal life, we can categorize people into two main groups: those who think they can achieve eternal life through rituals and practices and those who believe that eternal life is a gift bestowed solely by God.

Throughout Earth's history, various cultures have pursued longevity, immortality, or even divinity despite their inherently mortal nature. These aspirations have driven many individuals to subject themselves to extreme practices such as self-torture, isolation, and other rigorous rituals. People would undertake these often arduous and unpleasant practices with the belief that, upon passing, they would ascend to a higher realm and deities or achieve eternal life.

We find one such example in Jainism, a religion that originated in India. An Indian news article explained that:

> "Kanchan Devi Baid, an 82-year-old Jain woman, has decided to embrace death by opting for 'Santhara,' a practice of voluntary fasting in which a person stops the intake of food and water. This practice is called 'a festival of death' by the members of the Jain community. … Her granddaughter Nivedita Navlakkha said, '"Santhara" is part of our culture and is not new for us. I have heard that elders in our family have earlier observed this.' 'Seeing this in front of our eyes is not easy, but we are happy as she will attain "moksha" (salvation),' she added."[5]

The concept of immortality and godhood has captivated the human imagination to such an extent that countless Hollywood movies have portrayed characters who are immortal or ageless, or who ascend to God-like status upon death or through some other measures.

What if immortality could truly be attained through a formula or set of rituals? Would that mean anyone can have it simply by following these steps? If this were the case, it suggests that people could live however they please and then rely on these rituals to become immortal. This scenario would imply that a connection with the Creator and faith in God is unnecessary, as the rituals alone would suffice.

This idea is similar to certain atheists who believe that through some ritual they will live forever. Either way, the idea is dangerous. How?

Let's suppose that someone figures out a way to be immortal with or without believing in God. Would that actually be a good thing? This type of immortality doesn't assure us that it will be accessible only to good people, and neither does it assure us that anyone who gets access to it will become a righteous person.

While the concept of living forever may seem appealing at first, the implications of eternal life for everyone, regardless of their actions or intentions, raise complex moral questions. Imagine a world where individuals with malicious intent could perpetuate their harmful behaviors forever. In other words, there would be suffering for eternity—it's a troubling thought.

Though these are all assumptions and speculations, it's disheartening to consider the possibility of immortality or divinity achieved through some magical method. If that possibility were true, I might as well hope there is no eternity with or without God to avoid eternal suffering.

Now that we've imagined the results of receiving eternal life through rituals, we'll shift our focus to the second group who believe that eternal life is a unique gift solely bestowed by God, the Creator, and not something that can be achieved through human endeavor or inherent worth.

In the previous chapter on value, we established that a created being, by its very nature, cannot ascend to the status of God nor achieve eternal existence independently. This is because eternity is an attribute inherent to God alone. A being that is created is finite and bound by time, incapable of continuing into eternity without divine intervention.

While this eternal life is a free gift from the Creator to all human beings, some accept it, and some reject it. The acceptance of eternal life, as proposed by this belief system, is not based on human merit, status, or effort but on faith because it is a divine concept. This faith is a trust and belief in God's promise of eternal life and an acknowledgment of His sovereignty and grace. Here are two verses that speak about eternal life as a gift:

> *"The gift of God is eternal life in Christ Jesus our Lord"* (Romans 6:23).

> *"For by grace you have been saved through faith, and that not of yourselves; it is the gift of God, not of works, lest anyone should boast"* (Ephesians 2:8–9).

Honestly, comparing the two groups, it makes sense to believe that eternal life is not something we achieve through rituals or formula but is a free gift from the eternal God, available to everyone through faith. Because God is omniscient and omnipotent, He promises, *"Affliction will not rise up a second time"* (Nahum 1:9). The universe will remain a safe place forever.

However, faith in God for eternal life shouldn't be blind. It's essential to understand why attaining eternal life through Him is meaningful and leads to genuine anticipation. We don't want to feel coerced into entering heaven, nor do we envision an eternity of monotony. Instead, there must be something that makes the prospect of eternity both beautiful and fulfilling. What could that be? It's the beautiful character of God that gives us this anticipation.

Faith in Jesus to Receive Eternal Life

It's not the food we will eat, the golden streets we will walk, the perfect body, or any other benefits we will receive that make eternal life attractive. Instead, it's the understanding of God's character that truly makes eternity meaningful and something to eagerly anticipate. In this section, we'll explore four key elements of God's character that make eternal life not just desirable, but a beautiful and fulfilling experience. There are four main factors to consider:

1. A loving Judge who reserves eternal life for those who are righteous
2. A Creator with the ability to create diverse worlds to prepare a place for the righteous
3. A Friend whom the righteous would long to spend time with for eternity
4. A timeless God capable of bestowing eternal life

A Loving Judge

Can a judge truly be considered loving? A judge can be deemed truly loving when they demonstrate compassion and empathy towards those who have broken the law. By acknowledging the offender's willingness to repent, discerning the genuineness of their intentions, forgiving them, and granting them the opportunity to rectify their actions and abide by the law, the judge embodies love and understanding. Any other justification falls short of defining a loving judge.

There is a balance between justice and mercy that is often required in a judicial context. Indeed, a judge who forgives offenders without considering the consequences or without any basis for pardon may not be acting in the best interest of justice or the well-being of society. Similarly, a judge who rigidly adheres to the law without considering individual circumstances or showing any mercy also lacks compassion and understanding.

A loving judge, therefore, will strive to find a balance between justice and mercy, considering both the severity of the offense and the potential for rehabilitation. By doing so, the judge promotes accountability and respect for the law while also demonstrating care and empathy for those who come before the court.

To put this in perspective, have you ever heard of a judge named Frank Caprio? He is one of my favorite people and is known as the "Nicest Judge in the World." You might have seen him on short videos on different social media platforms. He is known for being a compassionate and an understanding judge who pardons people who have broken traffic laws.

This judge's approach of reasoning with the offenders and trying to empathize with their circumstances before deciding on a verdict is an example of a loving judge. Of course, he doesn't pardon everyone, but he does so for those he believes will turn in a new direction and live differently if pardoned.

In a world where justice often feels cold and distant, Judge Caprio considers the human element, listens to people's situations, and sets a positive example for judges.

Make no mistake, I'm not saying Judge Caprio is God, but he sure does give us a glimpse of God as a loving judge. God's love far exceeds human love. Therefore, His judgements are righteous and come out of compassion, empathy, justice, and love.

Many of us have come to see God as someone who is quick to punish people as soon as they commit a sin. This idea portrays Him as a tyrant eager to demonstrate His power through punishment. How many times have you told someone or been told, "You are going through this because you did something wrong, and God is punishing you for it"? If this were true, life would be miserable for all of us, as none of us are without fault. There would be no unrighteous individuals prospering on Earth, for God would have punished or even killed them.

However, there is no solid evidence in the Bible or in our present lives to support the idea that God is waiting to punish. In contrast, the Bible teaches in *2 Peter 3:9* that "the Lord is ... longsuffering toward us, not willing that any should perish but that all should come to repentance." So, how have we concluded that God is waiting to punish His creation? The concept of God solely being a punisher stems from misinterpretations or fear-based teachings originated by Satan and passed down through generations.

God is loving, forgiving, and compassionate. If it were not so, He would have destroyed Adam and Eve as soon as they sinned. God is a loving judge who balances justice and mercy. He empathizes with us through the life of Christ, understanding the depth of our temptations: *"For we do not have a High Priest who cannot sympathize with our weaknesses, but was in all points tempted as we are, yet without sin" (Hebrews 4:15).*

By the death of Jesus, God demonstrates compassion and offers us numerous opportunities for redemption, sparing us from ultimate death which is the second death: *"But God demonstrates His own love toward us, in that while we were still sinners, Christ died for us" (Romans 5:8).*

Through Jesus' resurrection, He forgives every sincere soul genuinely seeking His mercy for their sins: *"If we confess our sins, He is faithful and just to forgive us our sins and to cleanse us from all unrighteousness" (1 John 1:9).*

Those who have sinned out of ignorance are also granted forgiveness by God. He looks at how truthfully they have lived in accordance with the knowledge they were given. As stated in *Acts 17:30*, "Truly, these times of ignorance God overlooked."

God also affirms that sin and its consequences will be removed from the entire universe. This means unrepentant sinners, evil angels that tempt us, and Satan himself, the originator of sin, will all be burned in a lake of fire *(Revelation 20:10, 12; 21:8)*. God's love for us is so great that He evaluates each of our lives individually to guide us towards His kingdom. When you are willing to repent of your sins, God strengthens you to give up those sins and is willing to take you to heaven. But if you don't want to repent, then he removes you from the entire universe, putting an end to suffering. Now, that is a loving Judge we can freely worship!

This loving judge not only forgives, shows compassion, and makes us righteous but also loves us so deeply that He removes anything that causes fear, sorrow, or suffering. Below are some verses that testify to this loving Judge:

> *"The last enemy that will be destroyed is death"* (1 Corinthians 15:26).

> *"And God will wipe away every tear from their eyes; there shall be no more death, nor sorrow, nor crying. There shall be no more pain, for the former things have passed away"* (Revelation 21:4).

> *"I charge you therefore before God and the Lord Jesus Christ, who will judge the living and the dead at His appearing and His kingdom"* (2 Timothy 4:1).

So, how does knowing God is a loving Judge affect your faith practically?

Remember and Surrender: To help you develop your faith, always remember that God is in control. All the things you've gone through, are going through, or will go through in the future, are under His watchful eye. God will bring justice to all of it. God is a just God, so we don't have to seek justice on our own. Sometimes, we may feel the urge to control everything and solve all our problems by ourselves. But it's in those moments that we need to remember we are not alone in this world. The mighty God is with us! When you intentionally surrender your struggles to Him, your faith will grow, and you will experience a better quality of life.

We can gain the confidence in God because *Hebrews 10:30* says, *"For we know Him who said, 'Vengeance is Mine, I will repay,' says the Lord. And again, 'The LORD will judge His people.'"*

A Creator

The Bible provides evidence that Jesus is the Creator. *John 1:2–3, 14* tell us: "He was in the beginning with God. All things were made through Him, and without Him nothing was made that was made. … And the Word became flesh and dwelt among us, and we beheld His glory, the glory as of the only begotten of the Father, full of grace and truth."

The Bible also speaks about the existence of more than one world. *Hebrews 11:3* states, *"By faith we understand that the worlds were framed by the word of God, so that the things which are seen were not made of things which are visible."* This was written millennia before the invention of telescopes.

An article in the BBC Science Focus confirms what the above verse says,

"Recent estimates tell us that there could be as many as two trillion galaxies in the observable Universe."

"Two trillion galaxies is an estimate. Scientists haven't sat there and counted every single galaxy they've spotted in the known observable Universe. Instead, they have studied small sections of the Universe (equivalent size of a pinhead held at arm's length) and counted the galaxies in those fractions."[6]

Slowly but surely, scientific discoveries are aligning with references found in ancient biblical texts.

If Jesus, our God, is able to create different worlds by His words, then it gives us the assurance that He can create or prepare a place for us to live for eternity.

> Jesus assures in *John 14:1–4*, "Let not your heart be troubled; you believe in God, believe also in Me. In My Father's house are many mansions; if it were not so, I would have told you. I go to prepare a place for you. And if I go and prepare a place for you, I will come again and receive you to Myself; that where I am, there you may be also. And where I go you know, and the way you know."

Jesus prepares the heavenly place for us. But we need to remember that heaven is not an entitlement for Christians, but a gift from God to every single human being who chooses to cooperate with Him and live peaceful, joyful lives. While the entire universe will become a safe place once evil is abolished forever, we will dwell with Jesus in heaven.

But where do we start experiencing heaven? Heaven begins in this sinful world when you invite Jesus into your heart. Heaven is not merely a place, but a person—Jesus. Wherever Jesus is, that is where heaven exists. Everyone who has Jesus in their heart experiences a heavenly atmosphere.

We can observe this from the experiences of the apostles. When they saw heaven as merely a physical dwelling place, like a kingdom, they quarreled among themselves to decide who would sit closest to Jesus and tried to attain the highest rank next to Him. Similarly, when faced with trials at various times, including the night when Jesus was arrested by Roman soldiers, they all fled to preserve their lives.

Below are a couple examples that explicitly show the disciples' eagerness for external achievements:

> "And He [Jesus] said to her, 'What do you wish?' She [the mother of James and John] said to Him, 'Grant that these two sons of mine may sit, one on Your right hand and the other on the left, in Your kingdom'" (Matthew 20:21).

> "Now there was also a dispute among them [the disciples], as to which of them should be considered the greatest" (Luke 22:24).

But when they understood that having Jesus in their hearts is the heavenly experience, they were all willing to suffer, even unto death, because they were experiencing that heavenly atmosphere in a sinful world.

Peter and Paul express their heavenly experience of Christ dwelling in their hearts:

> "But rejoice to the extent that you partake of Christ's sufferings, that when His glory is revealed, you may also be glad with exceeding joy" (1 Peter 4:13).

> "I have been crucified with Christ; it is no longer I who live, but Christ lives in me; and the life which I now live in the flesh I live by faith in the Son of God, who loved me and gave Himself for me" (Galatians 2:20).

Another example to note is Stephen:

> *"But he [Stephen], being full of the Holy Spirit, gazed into heaven and saw the glory of God, and Jesus standing at the right hand of God, and said, 'Look! I see the heavens opened and the Son of Man standing at the right hand of God!' ... And they stoned Stephen as he was calling on God and saying, 'Lord Jesus, receive my spirit.' Then he knelt down and cried out with a loud voice, 'Lord, do not charge them with this sin.' And when he had said this, he fell asleep"* (Acts 7:55–56, 59–60).

The Spirit that made Stephen say these words, "Lord, do not charge them with this sin," is the same Spirit that made Jesus say, *"Father, forgive them, for they do not know what they do"* (Luke 23:34).

Do you see the similarity? Jesus not only helps us have a heavenly experience but also helps us to develop His character so that we can truly enjoy the heavenly mansions He's preparing for us.

We recognize that God has created multiple worlds, a concept supported by recent scientific findings. This gives us confidence in God's power to prepare a place for us to dwell for eternity. Additionally, God is actively working within us, if we allow Him, so that we can fully enjoy the heavenly dwelling He has prepared for us.

Acknowledge: The God who created the vast expanse of galaxies and countless beings also created you. He knows every detail about you—the good, the bad, the ugly—and still chooses you. This same God, who spoke the universe into existence, has the power to recreate and renew. He promises, *"I will give you a new heart and put a new spirit within you; I will take the heart of stone out of your flesh and give you a heart of flesh"* (*Ezekiel 36:26*). As you acknowledge the power of the Creator, He strengthens your faith.

Whenever you struggle to maintain your faith in God, you can echo the prayer of the man in *Mark 9:24*, *"Lord, I believe; help my unbelief!"*

> A powerful reminder to memorize and hold onto is *Isaiah 43:1*: *"But now, thus says the LORD, who created you, O Jacob, and He who formed you, O Israel: 'Fear not, for I have redeemed you; I have called you by your name; You are Mine.'"*

A Friend

Can God be a friend? Absolutely! In *John 15:15*, Jesus says, *"I have called you friends, for all things that I heard from My Father I have made known to you."* Jesus desires to spend time with us even while we're here on Earth. The question is, are we willing to spend time with Him? Developing a relationship with Jesus is very simple. We share with Him every day all our burdens, joys, dislikes, personal struggles, and even our frustrations—everything we wish to express. This is because He is deeply interested in our lives and listens to us with love and compassion.

Talking to Jesus is a privilege He has granted us. It's not a dead formality where we recite prayers mechanically every day or once a week, wondering if He's listening. Instead, it involves active engagement from both sides. While we may not hear His voice immediately as we do in conversations with other humans, this is where faith comes in. This faith connection is nurtured through reading the Bible, where we can find His words and teachings, and remaining open to His providential leading in our daily lives.

Developing a friendship with God can be a deeply rewarding and transformative experience. Just as any friendship requires time, effort, and communication, so does our relationship with Jesus. By taking the time to pray to Him regularly, we open up the channels of communication and strengthen our bond with Him.

You can share with Him all the struggles you have. You can confide in Him about all the joys you experience. You can seek His wisdom when you need understanding. You can ask for clarity and guidance in making decisions. You can bring any question or concern to Him, and you will receive an answer. Personally, I've received answers to various questions and situations in my life!

As we continue to grow in our relationship with Jesus, we discover that He's not just a distant figure to be worshipped but a true friend who walks alongside us, shares in our joys and sorrows, and provides us with strength and comfort. So, let's embrace this friendship with God wholeheartedly, knowing that He is always there for us, ready to listen and guide us every step of the way.

The below passage shows God's willingness to connect with us in all situations:

> *"Is anyone among you suffering? Let him pray. Is anyone cheerful? Let him sing psalms. Is anyone among you sick? Let him call for the elders of the church, and let them pray over him, anointing him with oil in the name of the Lord. And the prayer of faith will save the sick, and the Lord will raise him up. And if he has committed sins, he will be forgiven. Confess your trespasses to one another, and pray for one another, that you may be healed. The effective, fervent prayer of a righteous man avails much"* (James 5:13–16).

This is the experience we have on the earth right now. In the future when we live with Jesus in heaven—in the mansions He has gone to prepare for us in the New Jerusalem—He will dwell with us. We'll talk with Him face to face without any barrier. We can ask Him as many questions as we want, and He will patiently answer all our unanswered questions, doubts, and more.

All this is possible because Jesus made the provision for it. Jesus said, *"Greater love has no one than this, than to lay down one's life for his friends" (John 15:13).* With these words, Jesus defined the essence of true friendship and demonstrated it by laying down His life for us. This ultimate act of love not only exemplifies His friendship but also grants us the gift of eternal life. Our responsibility now is to accept this gift by embracing Jesus as our friend and placing our faith in Him.

Here's another promise from God to strengthen our faith:

> *"Then I, John, saw the holy city, New Jerusalem, coming down out of heaven from God, prepared as a bride adorned for her husband. And I heard a loud voice from heaven saying, 'Behold, the tabernacle of God is with men, and He will dwell with them, and they shall be His people. God Himself will be with them and be their God. And God will wipe away every tear from their eyes; there shall be no more death, nor sorrow, nor crying. There shall be no more pain, for the former things have passed away'" (Revelation 21:2–4).*

There are many promises in the Bible that may resonate deeply with you. As we choose to embrace these promises and stand firm on them, they become the foundation of our friendship with Jesus. Through this, we learn what it truly means to walk by faith and not by sight.

Connect with Interest: God deeply cares about your well-being.

He yearns to spend time with you, eager to hear about your happiest moments, deepest fears, uncomfortable situations, greatest achievements, and every detail of your life. As you seek His wisdom and counsel, rather than relying solely on your feelings or fears, you will experience a supernatural power working within you, enabling you to see His guidance. By connecting with Him by faith, you will witness God's hand leading you towards a quality life.

Your family, friends, mentors may fail, but God will never stop being your friend. The writer of *Psalm 73:25* prays to Him, *"Whom have I in heaven but You? And there is none upon earth that I desire besides You."*

An Eternal God

I could show you verses about Jesus being present from eternity past and living into eternity future—verses like Revelation 1:8: *"'I am the Alpha and the Omega, the Beginning and the End,' says the Lord, 'who is and who was and who is to come, the Almighty.'"*

But if you ask me to prove it, I won't be able to. I can prove Jesus as the loving Judge because of our continued existence in spite of our sins. I can prove Him as the Creator because nature testifies to it. I can testify to Jesus being our Friend, as can many others. However, I can't offer you direct proof of His eternal existence.

But I can tell you one thing: If I can believe in Jesus as the loving Judge, Creator, and Friend, then I have enough faith to believe that He is the eternal God. I have faith to believe that He has been present from eternity past and will be into eternity future. This is where faith must be sufficient to believe in Him.

Does the Bible talk about eternal life? Of course it does. Every single sincere Christian knows *John 3:16, "For God so loved the world that He gave His only begotten Son, that whoever believes in Him should not perish but have everlasting life.*" But this everlasting life would make no sense if we didn't believe in an eternal God. Our minds have to move above the level of human thinking and by faith contemplate the love and existence of God.

With all this being understood, I have confidence and faith in God that when the time is right, He will provide answers to all the questions we have. Questions such as how long God has been in existence, whether God will live forever, how long time has been in existence, where the ends of the universe are, and many more will be revealed in due time. Faith in God's plan and timing is essential.

We've explored how eternal life holds central importance in discussions of faith, representing the ultimate hope and goal for many. Have you ever wondered why this longing for eternity exists universally among humans, whether they accept Christianity, another religion, or even atheism? It's because the true Creator has instilled a sense of eternity within us, as stated in *Ecclesiastes 3:11, "He has made everything beautiful in its time. Also He has put eternity in their hearts."*

If God is ready to grant us eternal life, wouldn't He also be willing to provide us with a quality life on earth? Despite Jesus' acknowledgment of tribulation in this world *(John 16:33)*, He encourages us to hold onto faith even in the face of challenges. Through faith in Him, we can experience a quality life despite tribulations.

Hebrews 11:1 says, *"Now faith is the substance of things hoped for, the evidence of things not seen."* This verse beautifully articulates how faith serves as the foundation for our hopes and the conviction for the unseen. It's this unwavering trust that allows us to believe in the eternal existence of Jesus, the Alpha and the

Omega, the Beginning and the End.

Through faith, we can perceive the eternal nature of His being and find solace in His timeless presence in our lives, leading us to experience a quality of life that only faith in God can provide.

Don't you desire to experience Jesus personally? To dwell in heaven with your Creator, free from temptation, sin, sorrow, sickness, and death? This reality can be ours as long as we are guided by Him.

The current trajectory of the world suggests that it may not endure for much longer. All signs point to this. Though Jesus spoke of His imminent return two thousand years ago, recent events indicate that His coming is near.

I can't wait to see that beautiful face of Jesus who suffered for me. Horrifying stripes that He endured to redeem me. Cruel death to give me life. Don't you want to see your Creator who made it possible for you to live with your loved ones throughout eternity with Him?

So, let's hold fast to our faith, for in believing in Jesus as the loving Judge, Creator, and Friend, we also affirm our belief in His eternal divinity. This helps us develop a quality life. May our faith be a beacon of light guiding us through the mysteries of existence and leading us towards a deeper connection with the eternal God who has been, is, and will forever be.

Accept God's Gift: God offers eternal life to everyone, including you. It's your choice to accept this gift by faith, believing in Jesus and allowing Him to work within you *"both to will and to do for His good pleasure" (Philippians 2:13)*. As you permit God to transform you, His character will naturally be revealed in you. This means you don't have to struggle or pretend in your own strength. Think of it like a lamp; when it is lit, it automatically shines its light. It doesn't have to strive to illuminate.

Here's a verse worth memorizing to remind us to accept His eternal life: "Then Jesus spoke to them again, saying, *"I am the light of the world. He who follows Me shall not walk in darkness, but have the light of life"* (John 8:12).

Reflections:

1. Have you ever contemplated the possibility that there might not be a God present in the universe? What situations or circumstances prompt you to question the existence of God?
2. Reflect on all the chances God has given you so that He could work with you. What positive outcomes have you seen?
3. Write down experiences that have strengthened your faith. Read through these experiences whenever you are discouraged or doubting.
4. Why do you consider eternal life important?
5. Would you be willing to allow God to be your friend? If so, what personal matters or experiences would you be comfortable sharing with Him, the way you would with your closest friend?

References
1. "The Bible as History," National Museum of Natural History, Smithsonian Institution, https://csnradio.com/wp-content/uploads/2019/12/SmithsonianLetter-o.pdf.
2. "Using the Bible as Her Guide," *Philadelphia Trumpet,* April 2011, https://www.thetrumpet.com/8023-using-the-bible-as-her-guide.
3. "What Is the Statue in Nebuchadnezzar's Dream?" *AskAnAdventistFriend,* https://www.askanadventistfriend.com/understanding-the-bible/prophecy/what-is-the-statue-in-nebuchadnezzars-dream/.
4. Cyril J. Davey, *The Story of Sadhu Sundar Singh* (Chicago: Moody Press, 1963), 32–33.
5. "Gujarat Woman, 82, Begins Santhara, a Voluntary Fast Until Death," *NDTV,* May 16, 2019, https://www.ndtv.com/india-news/gujarat-jain-woman-82-begins-santhara-a-voluntary-fast-until-death-2038572/

amp/1.

6. Saunders, Toby, "How Many Galaxies Are in the Universe? A Lot More Than You'd Think," *BBC Science Focus,* July 25, 2023, science-focus.com/space/how-many-galaxies-are-in-the-universe/.

—◆—

Chapter Nine
LOVE
What Is Love?

––––– ✦ –––––

Love isn't merely a theoretical concept to study and understand. How do you really know what love is? How can you tell when you're in love? You can express your love through letters, poems, drawings, paintings, or acts of kindness, like cooking, taking your partner out, or giving gifts. But do these actions truly represent love, or are they merely expressions of it? Can't an acquaintance or even a random person perform these actions as well?

Imagine visiting a tourist spot where an artist sketches an exact picture of your wife. Does that mean he loves her? Or picture going to a friend's gathering, and your husband starts choking on food. A woman quickly performs the Heimlich maneuver to help him. Does this mean she loves him? Absolutely not! Your skills, talents, possessions, care, and actions are all replaceable. Then, how can you show your love? How can you say your love is unique?

Many people claim to love each other like no other, yet they break up with each other or even get divorced. Too many people give false promises and hopes in the name of love. I've seen people getting divorced after one year of marriage, ten years of marriage, and unbelievably, after thirty years of marriage. What happened there? Did they stop loving one another? Did their love move to someone else or something else? Is love like a wave that comes and goes?

When these people get into the next relationship, guess what! They express their love the same way. Didn't their previous love end despite years of "being in love"? Didn't they fall out of love? How do we know that this time it'll last "till death do us part"? Is there an assurance one could give? Are we supposed to live in fear that our partner might stop loving us at any moment?

Let's look at it from a different perspective. When you ask a man in a relationship, "What do you bring into the relationship or marriage that other men don't bring?" he may say "security," "fun," "loyalty," "leadership," "sexual fulfillment," "care," "love," or some other creative response. Is he the only one who can bring these to the relationship or marriage? I can assuredly tell you there are at least a million men in this world who can bring all of that into a relationship or marriage.

> *"Whether you're a man or a woman, you can't honestly say that your uniqueness or special ability is directly proportional to your love because there's always someone that can bring what you consider unique and special in yourself."*

When you ask a woman in a relationship, "What do you bring into the relationship or marriage that other women don't bring?" she may say "love," "care," "affection," "cooking," "sexual fulfillment," "support," "companionship," "respect," or some other creative response. Is she the only one who can bring these to the relationship or marriage? I can assuredly tell you there are at least a million women in this world that can bring all of these into a relationship or marriage.

Whether you're a man or a woman, you can't honestly say that your uniqueness or special ability is directly proportional to your love because there's always someone that can bring what you consider unique and special in yourself. Nevertheless, uniqueness is not what keeps people together in relationships. If it was, there wouldn't be people cheating on their partners. Using your uniqueness or special features as a basis for your prowess in love is not valid.

Imagine you discover a trait, something absolutely special that nobody else in the entire world can replicate. Then, something unfortunate occurs, and you lose that special trait, or you're unable to discover new traits anymore. Would it be right to say you no longer love your partner? Can your partner simply leave you, thinking you are no longer special? Is that really love?

In my high school, there was an extremely popular girl. Guys would gravitate towards her, and she consistently held their attention. Numerous individuals wanted to marry her. Their attraction primarily centered around her appearance, and let's be honest, how much does one know about love and life during high school anyway? Following high school, she married someone and gave birth to two children. Then, unexpectedly, a tragic accident occurred, resulting in brain damage that rendered her completely paralyzed. Subsequently, her husband abandoned her and their two children.

Can love be found in this situation? Do you believe he married her out of love? Even if his motive was love, what caused him to abandon the family after a few years? Did his love vanish? We can all understand that she became a burden to him, causing him to leave. Though she might've still been attractive, she couldn't give the same attention, care, and love as she once used to. His "love" proved to be superficial, leading him to abandon not only his wife but also their two children. Many people have abandoned their families in this same way and also in other scenarios. We can't label that as love. Then what is love?

Love doesn't arise solely from what we offer or are capable of doing. Love doesn't come because we have unique capabilities. If it did, then it would fade when we encounter something better than what we initially loved. It also becomes clear that love isn't even an emotion. If it were, it would ebb and flow like the tides of the sea. However, that's often how movies depict love worldwide—it's present for a while, then vanishes inexplicably. Imagine telling your partner that you love them, only for them to reply, "Today, I don't love you" due to a lack of emotional sentiment. Love isn't something that can be artificially cultivated. It can't be purchased or sold. It resists being coerced or manipulated. Then what, exactly, is love?

To understand love, we must turn to a source with extensive discussions on the subject—none other than the Holy Bible. The Bible provides teachings from children of God who explain how love is demonstrated. Throughout various stories, we see many examples of love in action. Moreover, an entire chapter, 1 Corinthians 13, is dedicated to love. We'll start with this chapter and see how Paul wrote about love:

> "Though I speak with the tongues of men and of angels, but have not love, I have become sounding brass or a clanging cymbal. And though I have the gift of prophecy, and understand all mysteries and all knowledge, and though I have all faith, so that I could remove mountains, but have not love, I am nothing. And though I

bestow all my goods to feed the poor, and though I give my body to be burned, but have not love, it profits me nothing" (1 Corinthians 13:1–3).

In the above passage, Paul speaks about how, without love, everything else we possess is useless.

"Love suffers long and is kind; love does not envy; love does not parade itself, is not puffed up; does not behave rudely, does not seek its own, is not provoked, thinks no evil; does not rejoice in iniquity, but rejoices in the truth; bears all things, believes all things, hopes all things, endures all things" (1 Corinthians 13:4–7).

Here, he explains the expression of love.

"Love never fails. But whether there are prophecies, they will fail; whether there are tongues, they will cease; whether there is knowledge, it will vanish away. For we know in part and we prophesy in part. But when that which is perfect has come, then that which is in part will be done away. When I was a child, I spoke as a child, I understood as a child, I thought as a child; but when I became a man, I put away childish things. For now we see in a mirror, dimly, but then face to face. Now I know in part, but then I shall know just as I also am known. And now abide faith, hope, love, these three; but the greatest of these is love" (1 Corinthians 13:8–13).

Paul beautifully describes the value of love but doesn't answer our question, "What is love?"

However, the apostle John gives the perfect definition for our quest. In 1 John 4:8, 16, he answers, *"God is love."* Alas! Now we have the answer to the question, "What is love?" When you experience God, you experience love. You can't experience love without God. You can't separate love from God. The whole world experiences this love, but most are ignorant to the fact that it is God. But some experience love and recognize that only God can give a unique and pure love. Love is an experience that words can't explain! Love is a person! God is love!

Love is a fascinating subject to study. People of all walks of life have researched and come up with different ideas, but without the Holy Bible, no one can explain what love is. Even Satan knows what love is and experienced it for a long time while he was still Lucifer. He knows the impact that love can have on each individual, and therefore, he doesn't want people to recognize God's love because when people recognize it, they will want more, and if they want more, they must come to Jesus. There is no other place where one can get the supreme experience of love.

But why do I say everyone has experienced God's love in this world? You might be sick, and the loving God isn't healing you, or you're struggling with something, and God is not helping you come out of the struggle. You might have even felt that no one has ever loved you from birth because your parents abandoned you, you were abused wherever you went, people mistreated you, or your spouse cheated on you. How can you know God loves you? Let me ask you a counter question: How do you know God hasn't loved you through all that you've been through? How do you know God Himself hasn't suffered with all that you've been through? These questions are tricky to answer without understanding how God works.

To better understand, we need to see the big picture. Seeing this big picture will help us realize the abundance of grace and love that God has given us from a young age.

Can you wholeheartedly say that you've never sinned? No honest person would answer yes to this question. If we all confess that we have sinned, as the apostle Paul said—*"for all have sinned and fall short of the glory of God"* (Romans 3:23)—then we are all doomed to eternal death. *"For the wages of sin is death"* (Romans 6:23). Then how are we still alive? Do you remember the memory verse that you learned growing up? *"For God so loved the world that He gave His only begotten Son"* (John 3:16, emphasis added). God expressed His love *"while we were still sinners" (Romans 5:8)* by giving us His Son, His only Son.

Through the death of Jesus on the cross, we see God's love for us because only His death made it possible for grace to abound where sin abounded *(Romans 5:20)*. Thus, we sinners are given more opportunities to be saved. Jesus experienced our pain (not having an earthly father and experiencing ridicule, betrayal, abuse, stripes, abandonment, grief, mental struggles, discrimination, prejudice, loneliness, isolation, political upheaval, persecution, etc.) in a sinful world and paid our debt so that we can live a life freely revealing hope in His love.

This shows that God empathizes with us and suffers along with us. However, as humans, our sight is limited, and we often feel that every challenge must be immediately resolved to assure ourselves of God's love. God sees the bigger picture and acts in our best interest, even when it may seem like He is not responding or helping us in a particular situation.

God's Love as a Pregnant Mother

Imagine a mother who is pregnant. She takes special care of her baby in the womb, attending regular prenatal checkups to monitor the baby's development and her own health. She maintains a nourishing diet, stays well-hydrated, exercises, and educates herself about childbirth. She also avoids harmful habits, such as smoking, even secondhand smoke, alcohol, caffeine, exposure to toxic chemicals, and heavy lifting. The mother's dedication to her well-being during pregnancy is unwavering.

During this time, the mother doesn't fret over whether her baby will love her in return. Of course, she hopes for love, but she isn't preoccupied with it. Her actions aren't motivated by expectations of what she might gain in the future. She provides the best care she can because the baby is hers. She is driven by love and doesn't expect reciprocity. The baby, in its infancy, cannot reciprocate this love. It receives care, affection, and tenderness without the capacity to respond similarly. This love is pure and selfless, akin to God's love for us.

God's love is unconditional, irrespective of the choices we make in our lives. While God hopes for our love in return and for us to love others as He loves us, He never forces it. Even so-called discipline serves as a path to our own growth and improvement. Mistakes become valuable lessons on our journey to becoming better individuals. Love, at its core, is about giving without expecting anything in return. It's about giving, even when the recipient may not accept it readily.

God's Love in Marriage

All humans are created to both receive and give love because *"God created man in His image" (Genesis 1:27)*. This implies that, as God is love, He has bestowed upon us a portion of His love. This includes the sacred union of marriage, symbolized by the union of Adam and Eve when God joined them in matrimony.

It's a beautiful experience when human love is founded on God's love. Before sin, Adam and Eve's love was one such love. Their love was in perfect harmony with God's love while they still maintained their individuality. This harmony of a *"threefold cord" (Ecclesiastes 4:12)* was broken as soon as sin entered. But still, God's great love has made provisions to bring the threefold cord back into harmony.

While living in Maine, I distinctly recall my brother sharing these words of wisdom with me: "Martin, there may be ten girls who are compatible with you and share the same values, but God has reserved only one for you." How true was this statement! It opened my eyes to a profound truth that many overlook.

God places that special love in one heart for you and vice versa. While you are free to marry anyone you like and there may be many whom you are compatible with, attracted to, develop feelings for, and share common values with, the special connection exists uniquely with one person.

If you have been surrendering your heart and listening to His voice, God will be developing higher qualities of character within you and also developing those qualities in your future partner. As you give it time, you will see God's plan unfolding, guiding your hearts towards each other. Even in those higher qualities of character, you will see a match. This experience was definitely true for me and my wife.

However, this doesn't mean that this union will be perfect and without any issues. In Adam and Eve's union, it was God who brought them together, and they were a perfect couple, a perfect match. But as soon as sin entered, their marriage took a turn. They started blaming each other and eventually blamed God for their own faults.

Does this sound similar to today? How many times do we see husbands and wives blaming each other constantly about something while they could very well build up and support each other? This is all due to the entrance of sin into the world. We all have our weaknesses, quirks, and ways of living that may tempt the other person to become annoyed or irritated. The same is true in every relationship, whether between siblings or friends: both parties have to put in work.

Jesus gives us this precious gift of love that is neither irrational nor ignorant. His love never destroys human love; instead, it refines, purifies, and makes it noble. Our love alone can't bear good results unless it's combined with God's love—thus, the purpose of a threefold cord *(Ecclesiastes 4:12)*.

> *"True love is calm, deep, wise, and discerning, attracted by qualities beyond externals. A successful marriage can only be achieved when we patiently surrender it to God along with our weaknesses."*

In such a home, love reigns and finds expression in thoughtful acts of kindness and courtesy. Christ's grace can unite hearts in heavenly bonds that endure through tests and trials, allowing the couple to reach God's ideal for them.

Thus, we learn how to love and respect each other in this union. It's the love of God that not only brings us together but also keeps us together.

Debbie and I became good friends with a couple at church, and as we learned about their history, we were amazed. Eleven years into their marriage, in 2004, Don suffered a terrible accident at work. Lying motionless in a ditch, waiting to be found, he realized he was paralyzed. Despite his dire situation, he felt a profound peace in dying but also told God that if there was more for him to do, he asked God to spare his life.

Soon, Don was discovered and rushed to the hospital. He was hospitalized for five months, and on several occasions, it seemed like he wouldn't make it. For two of those months, he was in the ICU. During that time, a psychologist informed Don that he should expect his wife, Cheri, to leave him, as it happens more often than not in such situations. Don confidently responded, "It won't happen because we are Christians." The psychologist argued that it wouldn't make a difference, but Don remained steadfast.

Cheri was unwavering in her commitment, clearly stating that she would stay with Don for the rest of their lives. In October 2023, they celebrated 30 years of marriage. They acknowledged that it hadn't always been easy, especially enduring the traumatic aftermath of the accident for the next twenty years. Yet, they confessed that it was God's grace that drew them closer to

Him and to each other, allowing them to happily declare their marriage a success.

The love they share stands as a testament to what God can do. Their story demonstrates the divine love that not only brings people together but also keeps them together.

Sometimes, people rush into marriages that may not be in line with God's will. However, it's important to remember that God's love for you remains unchanged despite the choices you make. If you find yourself in such a situation, know that God can still work in your life and in the life of your spouse to bring you closer and help you become more compatible. The road ahead may be more challenging than if you had married in His will, but as long as you both remain obedient to God's guidance, your marriage can still thrive and improve with time. So, take heart and trust in God's plan for your life.

Marriage is a lifelong commitment that is meant to be cherished and nurtured. For some, finding the right partner may come easily, but for others, it may take some time. However, as per God's will, once you find the person you want to spend the rest of your life with, it's important to hold on tight and never let go. But what if unforeseen circumstances arise? What if the person you married passes away or you experience a divorce? In these situations, trust in God's plan and know that if it is in His plan, He will guide you toward another person in whom He will place His love, bringing love and attraction into your life. Trust His time and way. Don't rush or become desperate but allow God to heal your wounds. Rest in His love for you.

Remember that marriage is a sacred institution established by

God for a reason. Unfortunately, Satan wants to destroy this institution, make it seem less important, and mar its significance. We must remain steadfast in our commitment to our spouse, and divorce should never be an option unless it's biblically justified. Let's honor and respect the covenant of marriage God has given us.

But what is the significance of a marriage union? It's a symbolic representation of Christ's relationship with His church. Passages like *Revelation 19:7–9* and *Matthew 25:1–13* give the analogy of the marriage union to describe the union of Christ and the church. *Ephesians 5:25–27* also makes it clear:

"Husbands, love your wives, just as Christ also loved the church and gave Himself for her, that He might sanctify and cleanse her with the washing of water by the word, that He might present her to Himself a glorious church, not having spot or wrinkle or any such thing, but that she should be holy and without blemish."

Do you remember how much importance God placed on the sacrificial offerings in the Old Testament? Those sacrifices pointed to the ultimate sacrifice of Christ on the cross. Similarly, God places importance on the marriage union because it represents Christ's union with the church. Thus, it is very sacred! The only way to break this sacred union is by committing adultery—choosing Satan's frivolous enticing and pleasures over Christ's true love and faithfulness.

The wedding day procession is a familiar sight all over the world and in most religions. The groom stands at the altar, waiting for his bride to join him. But have you ever wondered where this tradition comes from?

Interestingly, the roots of this custom can be traced back to the very first wedding in the Garden of Eden. According to *Genesis 2:22*, Adam was created first, and then Eve was created and brought to him. This mirrors the modern-day practice of the father walking his daughter down the aisle to give her away to her future husband.

Furthermore, this wedding procession is also reflected in the biblical account of the second coming of Christ. *Revelation 19:7* pictures Christ ready to receive His bride, the church, when she is ready.

Thus, this wedding tradition not only reflects the beautiful story of Adam and Eve but also serves as a reminder of the eternal love story between Christ and His church.

Even though God places a lot of importance on marriage, singleness is also valued in the Bible. Unfortunately, it is often misunderstood in today's society and viewed as a negative thing. But some individuals are called by God to be single for a specific purpose—to bless others. This calling can either last for a period of time or for a lifetime.

In fact, we find examples of such individuals in the Bible, such as Jeremiah, Daniel, and Paul. Note that these individuals were not single by accident or by chance, but rather because God had a specific purpose for their singleness. As we navigate through life, we should remember that singleness can be a calling and a blessing too, just like marriage.

When it comes to love in marriage, remember that it's not what we do that brings us together and keeps us together. It isn't our muscles or looks or talent or riches that make this beautiful union happen. The moment you think your partner likes you because of what you possess, you are opening the door to potential infidelity. If your partner is with you because of what you possess, then when they find someone better than you or someone who has something bigger to offer, you are more likely to be cheated on. One shouldn't marry someone based on their possessions or looks.

When you express this superficial *"love"* without Christ, you end up with a counterfeit or self-centered love that can result in hurt expectations, emotional stress, damaged relationships, unfulfilled connections, tolerance, hurt feelings, resentment, wasted time, a lack of intimacy, poor mental health, or the potential to become a victim or even prey. In contrast, when you experience true love, you are compelled to share it with others because of its magnitude and the profound impact it has on you, regardless of the outcome.

Therefore, God must be the one who brings us together and keeps us together. That's what makes each marriage unique and irreplaceable. When your bond is that strong, you can live in peace and not feel insecure even when a prettier lady passes by your husband or a richer man passes by your wife. It's because of this heavenly love that the soul is purified, relationships are strengthened, and darkness is destroyed. This love gives without expecting anything in return and brings out the best of emotions. It's affectionate and caring, always wanting the best for the partner. With this love, there's hope for the future and a quality life. The heavenly bond is stronger than any other attraction, and it's what makes a marriage truly remarkable.

So far, we have seen love from the perspective of marriage and romantic relationships, and how without God's love there can't be a holy union. However, God's love is not limited to romantic relationships; it's essential for all of our relationships to be healthy. In the next sections, we'll see how God's love influences our love for others and our love for God Himself.

Love Others, Especially Your Enemies

To love others is not an easy task. There will always be difference in opinions, work styles, and personality. However, overcoming these challenges and maintaining a healthy relationship is only possible with mature and godly love. No one can generate this type of love on their own.

It's easy to show love and friendship to those you don't have issues with. Jesus points this out, *"For if you love those who love you, what reward have you? Do not even the tax collectors do the same? And if you greet your brethren only, what do you do more than others? Do not even the tax collectors do so?"* (Matthew 5:46–47) These people can be good friends, family members, or those who have the same beliefs as you.

What about those people who dislike you because they are jealous of you, don't share the same beliefs as you, or mock and bully you? Jesus did say, *"And because lawlessness will abound, the love of many will grow cold"* (Matthew 24:12). As the months and years pass by, we can see this prophecy becoming more and more real. While social media has many positive uses, it's also a platform for cyberbullying and online harassment, often carried out under the anonymity of the internet. Do we need to love these people?

What about bad neighbors, corrupt spiritual leaders, people of other religions, criminals, and everyone else causing harm to society and affecting you and your loved ones? Do we need to love these people as well?

> *"Theoretically, it's easy to say we need to love our enemies, but is it really doable when it comes to the practice? Can you and I really love our enemies in those circumstances? No! It's impossible for us to love them."*

Jesus' counsel is *"But I say to you, love your enemies, bless those who curse you, do good to those who hate you, and pray for those who spitefully use you and persecute you" (Matthew 5:44)*.

Theoretically, it's easy to say we need to love our enemies, but is it really doable when it comes to the practice? Can you and I really love our enemies in those circumstances? No! It's impossible for us to love them. However, we can do all things through Christ who strengthens us *(Philippians 4:13)*.

Those who accept God's love will allow Him to do good works through them *(Philippians 2:13)*, resulting in wholehearted love for others, including their enemies. They are not ashamed by others' mockery of their faith, nor are they offended by others' actions. Their love remains constant in every circumstance because they receive this unshakable love from God.

This also doesn't mean they condone the wrong actions of others. They address the issues with Christlike love and wisdom. As God's love works in you, it will help you extend that love to others.

Paul encourages us *"as the elect of God, holy and beloved ... bearing with one another, and forgiving one another, if anyone has a complaint against another; even as Christ forgave you, so you also must do"* (Colossians 3:12–13).

Peter reminds us to not return *"evil for evil or reviling for reviling, but on the contrary blessing, knowing that you were called to this, that you may inherit a blessing"* (1 Peter 3:9).

Finally, John emphasizes that *"if someone says, 'I love God,' and hates his brother, he is a liar; for he who does not love his brother whom he has seen, how can he love God whom he has not seen?"* (1 John 4:20)

If we truly believe in God and receive His love, our actions will reflect it—not as a pretentious superficial act but through the deep working of the Holy Spirit. In other words, you don't have to force yourself to love someone; as you let God work in you, the love will be revealed naturally.

Loving your spouse, romantic partner, and others works when you believe in God. But what if you or someone you know doesn't believe in God? Can love still be present when God doesn't exist? We'll find out.

Freedom in God's Love

Some individuals crave absolute freedom, even rebelling against or denying the existence of God. They see biblical beliefs as *"restrictions."* They want to live their lives with absolute freedom and not be bound by biblical principles even if those principles are for our good. Unfortunately, they fail to see that God's love is freedom indeed.

For them, life is viewed as a simple cycle of birth, life, and death without a greater purpose. Interestingly, when atrocities occur, these same individuals, who believe in absolute freedom, are often the ones who vehemently protest and cry out for justice. How can we recognize injustice? It's because *"the love of God has been poured out in our hearts" (Romans 5:5)* that we can distinguish right from wrong. This divine love compels us to seek for justice, even for people we don't know. This inherent love from God also extends our compassion to animals.

If we accept the idea that there is no God, then who makes the call on what constitutes an atrocity and what doesn't? How do we even define what justice is? Everyone will have their own reasoning and justification, and nothing can be called right or wrong. This means criminals can't be condemned for their actions since they have the same freedom as everyone else.

In this case, we can't even have a social construct because it will raise a question as to why one individual or even a group should dictate another's decisions or actions. In such a scenario, survival of the fittest is the only guiding principle, leaving no room for claims of right or wrong. Is this how we want to live our lives? Consider a society built on the principle of absolute freedom and the belief that there is no God. In such a society, individuals would be free to act as they please with no regard for the consequences of their actions. Murder, theft, and other forms of criminal behavior would be rampant since there would be no moral guidance to define right from wrong. This would lead to chaos and anarchy, with each individual looking out only for themselves.

Wait a minute! Didn't we have people do such things in the past? Does this mean that what individuals like Adolf Hitler, Idi Amin, and Benito Mussolini did was perfectly fine? Without an objective moral standard, we can't even consider them as criminals or dictators because who are we to judge and label their actions as wrong?

In such a world, those who have blessed millions of people—such as the Staines family, Mother Theresa, and Oskar Schindler—would be seen on the same level as those who have hurt millions. Is that what you agree with? No! We all agree that we can differentiate between good and bad people.

This ability to distinguish arises from the love of God within us. Thus, it is God's love that provides us with true freedom and a moral compass. If we pursue freedom outside of this divine love, it often results in one person's freedom infringing upon another's. Without God, the source of love, there is no true freedom.

Social Media Mockery

I've encountered unkind comments, mockery, and ridicule on social media directed at those who believe in God. Those who criticize believers often ask questions like, "If God is love, why does He allow people to die unfairly?" or "Why doesn't your God prevent natural disasters?" They may even make statements like, "I'll believe in God when He stops a plane with 500 people from crashing."

Although these questions are valid, they can be difficult to answer, especially in times of personal tragedy. However, those who are open-minded can find hope and happiness in the answers.

There are valid explanations for these difficult questions and understanding them can bring peace to those who seek it.

So, how can we justify when tragedy strikes, and God doesn't save? The moment we accept God is present, we must also acknowledge that God's power transcends our understanding and reaches far beyond our limited human lives. Life is not just about the short time we have on earth, but also about a greater purpose that we may not fully comprehend now.

Unfortunately, people who see this life as the ultimate reality cannot fathom a life beyond this. Thus, when people are not saved from a tragedy right away, they resort to believing God is not present because God would have saved them.

God's Love Is the Answer!

In this temporary life, those who pass away tragically are not completely gone. *Revelation 22:12* tells us that God carefully evaluates their lives and rewards them accordingly. Those who accepted God's gift of eternal life will no longer experience death, sorrow, or crying, as revealed in *Revelation 21:4*. This means there will be no more difficulties, tragedies, or unjust happenings. On the other hand, those who have led a terrible life and were given multiple chances to repent but never took them will be subjected to the consequences of their actions and will ultimately cease to exist. It seems only fair that those who refused to change their ways and intentionally caused harm to others should face such a fate. This will be the moment when all the injustices committed for temporary selfish gain will be punished, and all the righteous deeds will be rewarded with eternal gifts. Sadly, people often overlook God's interventions to protect individuals on the brink of death. These interventions are a manifestation of His mercy, allowing those individuals another opportunity to live a life of repentance. God, in His infinite wisdom, knows precisely who requires more time to turn their life around. Although God provides multiple opportunities for repentance for all, some may need to undergo extreme circumstances to facilitate their transformation. These challenging experiences may be the only way to push them towards leading a better life.

All that God does is counted in His infinite love. Whether it's Adolf Hitler or Mother Theresa, God sees their hearts and rewards them accordingly. Whether someone has lived a full life or died prematurely, God rewards them according to how they lived because their lives show whether they have truly received God's gift of salvation.

God doesn't want anyone to perish and is willing to forgive and transform your life no matter the past. Those who accept God's gift of eternal life will be saved from sin, and for those who do not, death is the result.

Supreme Love in Heaven

My brother's friend was looking forward to a business trip to Malaysia, where he planned to stay for a few months. However, upon his return to India, he shared that he was disappointed with his experience. When asked why, he explained that the laws in Malaysia were too strict for his liking. He missed the freedom he had in India to spit or throw things wherever he pleased. While this behavior may seem unsanitary to some, there is a valuable lesson to be learned here.

Similar to this friend, some reject the idea of being bound by laws and instead choose to live with complete freedom. For them, the thought of heaven bound by a law of love may seem like a difficult or even undesirable place to be. However, this law of love actually provides the ultimate freedom.

Would those who refuse to repent and continue to want to harm others truly be happy in such a place? It seems unlikely that they'd be able to fully embrace and appreciate the true nature of heaven, which is built on love, kindness, and compassion for all. Therefore, out of His great love, God will bring an end to their existence. This also means that God will bring an end to the suffering, pain, and injustice.

On a positive note, we are drawn closer to God as we study His free gift of salvation and eternal life. We desire to love Him because He is willing to forgive us when we ask for pardon. We desire to love Him because He brings justice in His judgment. We desire to love Him because He gives us the love for our spouse and others, including our enemies, so that we can have the best quality of life.

In heaven, we will reunite with our loved ones forever. Whether we have lost them due to tragic accidents, health issues, or simply because of old age, we will all come together in a peaceful and flawless setting. This makes us want to love God even more.

How could we not love such a God! *"We love Him because He first loved us" (1 John 4:19).*

In this place called heaven, we will be reunited with our loved ones and will never experience the pain of separation again. More importantly, we will never be separated from our Savior,

Jesus Christ. It will be a utopia, where perfect love reigns, emanating solely from a divine source. A love that surpasses all understanding, a supreme love that can only be found in Jesus, will be given and received by all.

Reflections:
1. Does your life reflect Christ and His peace in your heart?
2. Has your life been a blessing to everyone, rather than just those you love?
3. If you were to die in an unexpected tragedy, do you have peace with God? Is there a legacy you are leaving behind for people to follow?
4. What steps will you take from today onward to cultivate a life filled with love?
5. Write down ten things around you that make you feel loved. (These could include nature, family, friends, opportunities, etc.) Acknowledge them and thank God for them.

If you have come this far, congratulations! I pray that what you've read has brought revival in your heart and made you determined to seek a quality life.

—◆—

CONCLUSION

When a new car is being developed, it undergoes a series of rigorous tests to ensure it performs well in different settings and conditions prior to its availability for purchase. These tests are part of a meticulous process to ensure the car is fully functional and suitable for everyday use. Should any issues arise during testing, the company won't proceed with releasing the product. Instead, they'll diligently address and resolve the issues before moving forward. Throughout this process, patience is paramount. Rushing to release a product with unresolved issues can pose safety risks and compromise overall quality.

Likewise, in life, we all go through times when we are tested in different aspects. Whether we are waiting to find a spouse, or someone cheated us in business, or we are dealing with trauma from our past, we are being tested. God allows us to go through this meticulous process of testing.

You might wonder why, and I don't blame you. From a human standpoint, it might seem unnecessary, and we might even think God is cruel because He is letting us go through all these tests instead of keeping us safe from everything. But is He cruel?

In life, we are like cars manufactured by God. However, because of the enemy, Satan, who caused a malfunction, we started breaking down easily at every pit and bump along the road.

Only God can give us the nine basic yet essential components—joy, peace, patience, kindness, virtue, humility, temperance, faith, and love—necessary for a smooth and safe journey. Just as cars cannot assemble their basic components on their own, we can't create these qualities by ourselves.

One of the two vital components, as we've seen, is determination. It provides the drive that keeps us moving forward in the pursuit of a quality life. Just as a car can't move without its driver turning on the engine and controlling its movements, we need determination to guide us.

And what about the other indispensable factor, the fuel? If you haven't guessed it already, it's the Holy Spirit. God gives us the Holy Spirit as we need it and as we request it. The Holy Spirit acts as the fuel that enables us to succeed in our journey to a quality life.

The manufacturer, God, allows us to undergo rigorous tests and trials so that He can help us become a quality product—fully functional and perfectly suitable for heaven. He can't take us to heaven without our cooperation in His work within us. Imagine if a car manufacturer released a model for sale that consistently malfunctioned; it would cause safety hazards for those traveling in it and for others around.

Similarly, God can't bring us to heaven without fully working in us, as we wouldn't find ourselves comfortable or safe there and might even pose a danger to others. Therefore, God molds our character through tests and trials on this earth, showing us the importance of relying on Him rather than on self.

The most significant distinction between a car and a human being is the ability to exercise free will and make our own choices. While cars operate according to their design and mechanical functions, humans possess free will, enabling them to make choices that shape their lives and destinies.

God doesn't force us to go to heaven; He extends His invitation to all with His everlasting love, even to the worst sinner on this earth. He never coerces us into believing in Him or following Him but gives us the opportunity to make that choice freely.

The people who have forced Christianity on others have set a wrong example of who Christ is and how His love works. From the beginning, God has always drawn His creation to Him with love and not force.

Freedom in God's Love

One morning, I was lying in bed, and my wife was planning to get ready for the day. However, I wanted her to lie down next to me—not to engage in any activities or even to speak but simply to be by my side because I felt an overflow of love for her in my heart. Having her next to me brought me immense joy.

That's when I realized something important: if she had forced me to fall in love with her or to marry her, I wouldn't have felt attracted. Throughout our courtship and in our marriage, she has given me the freedom to spend time with my brother and friends. She has given me the freedom to go on a drive by myself if and when I wanted to. She has given me freedom in my weight loss journey, not forcing me to do what I needed to do but instead empowering me by letting me choose what I want to do. She has simply offered pointers on what works and what doesn't.

As she continued to give me freedom and didn't smother me with *"love"* and codependency, the more I wanted to spend time with her. This is true for all of us! In relationships that aren't dysfunctional, we love each other more because there is freedom in love.

Similarly, God grants us freedom. He never forces us to follow Him. It's our choice whether to accept Him or not, but He draws us closer to Him with His love so that we can develop trust in Him, enjoy the journey, and align our will with God's. If we choose not to, He respects that as well.

Satan's First Deception About God

In the Great Commission, Jesus said, *"'All authority has been given to Me in heaven and on earth. Go therefore and make disciples of all the nations, baptizing them in the name of the Father and of the Son and of the Holy Spirit, teaching them to observe all things that I have commanded you; and lo, I am with you always, even to the end of the age.' Amen"* (Matthew 28:18–20).

Note that Jesus said to make disciples, baptize them, and teach them. These verbs outline the specific mission work Jesus has given His disciples from His time until the end of the world. Did you notice something? Nowhere does He say to engage in debates with nonbelievers, force people into Christianity, or threaten them with eternal hellfire.

Unfortunately, Satan has led people in the wrong direction, causing them to preach fear, engage in debates, or coerce others into Christianity. Nowhere in the Bible will you find God forcing people to bow down to Him. On the contrary, Satan tried to force Jesus to bow down and worship him:

"Again, the devil took Him [Jesus] up on an exceedingly high mountain, and showed Him all the kingdoms of the world and their glory. And he said to Him, 'All these things I will give You if You will fall down and worship me.' Then Jesus said to him, 'Away with you, Satan! For it is written, "You shall worship the LORD your God, and Him only you shall serve""" (Matthew 4:8–10).

Throughout the Bible, we see examples of God inviting and calling people to worship Him, but His call is always presented as a choice. Individuals are given the freedom to respond to God's invitation according to their own will. Here are a few passages that highlight this aspect:

"I call heaven and earth as witnesses today against you, that I have set before you life and death, blessing and cursing; therefore choose life, that both you and your descendants may live; that you may love the LORD your God, that you may obey His voice, and that you may cling to Him, for He is your life and the length of your days; and that you may dwell in the land which the LORD swore to your fathers, to Abraham, Isaac, and Jacob, to give them" (Deuteronomy 30:19–20).

"And if it seems evil to you to serve the LORD, choose for yourselves this day whom you will serve, whether the gods which your fathers served that were on the other side of the River, or the gods of the Amorites, in whose land you dwell. But as for me and my house, we will serve the LORD" (Joshua 24:15).

These passages emphasize the personal choice and freedom God has given us. While God desires worship from His creation, He does not force it from anyone but rather invites people to come to Him willingly and acknowledge His sovereignty, goodness, and love. Genuine worship stems from a relationship with God and is expressed through love, reverence, and obedience.

Satan's Second Deception About God

Satan takes things to one extreme by presenting God as someone who coerces and threatens with hellfire to draw people closer to Him. Satan also takes it to the other extreme by suggesting that we can do whatever we want and still make it to heaven if we just believe in Jesus.

This is why some Christians argue that belief in Jesus alone and His merit—and not our actions—is what secures our place in heaven. While this statement holds truth, it raises the question, shouldn't our lives serve as a witness to others that we truly believe in Jesus?

Wait a minute, don't Satan and his angels believe in Jesus? They absolutely do!

> *"When He [Jesus] had come to the other side, to the country of the Gergesenes, there met Him two demon-possessed men, coming out of the tombs, exceedingly fierce, so that no one could pass that way. And suddenly they cried out, saying, 'What have we to do with You, Jesus, You Son of God? Have You come here to torment us before the time?'" (Matthew 8:28–29)*

CONCLUSION

Did you notice how the demons acknowledged Jesus? They said, *"You Son of God."* This proves that even the evil angels, also known as demons, believe in Jesus. Then, how should our belief in Jesus be different than those of demons?

In James chapter 2, the author speaks on how faith will be revealed in works:

> *"But someone will say, 'You have faith, and I have works.' Show me your faith without your works, and I will show you my faith by my works. You believe that there is one God. You do well. Even the demons believe—and tremble! But do you want to know, O foolish man, that faith without works is dead?" (verses 18–20)*

James continues the thought using the examples of Abraham and Rahab. Abraham showed his faith by being willing to offer Isaac his son on the altar according to God's command, and Rahab showed her faith by protecting the life of the messengers from the king of Jericho.

They both revealed their faith through works. James concludes with a balanced thought that faith and works are intertwined, and one can't be present without the other:

> *"For as the body without the spirit is dead, so faith without works is dead also" (verse 26).*

While belief in Jesus is essential for salvation, the way we live our lives should naturally reflect it. Our actions, attitudes, and choices should align with the teachings of Jesus, serving as a testimony of our faith to others. Simply claiming to believe in Jesus while continuing to live in a manner contrary to His teachings undermines the credibility of our faith and contradicts the essence of true belief.

Thus, faith and belief in Jesus are not just words; they are revealed through our works. These works are the working of the Holy Spirit in and through us. My words, my actions, and my deeds are all influenced by the Holy Spirit, and others will be able to see that.

God continues to demonstrate His love for us not by condemning us for our sins *(John 8:11)* but by cleansing us and leading us to repentance *(Matthew 9:13)*.

It's Satan who tries to expose our sins, condemn us, and accuse us. He hates us all, even if we claim to be on his side, and that is a sign that he hates himself.

Jesus knew that Judas was a thief *(John 12:4–6)*, but He never exposed him for stealing money. Instead, Jesus worked with Judas to win him with love. Even when Judas kissed Jesus in betrayal, Jesus called him *"friend."* Though Jesus knew that Judas did it to betray Him, Jesus was still trying to work in Judas's heart to bring him to repentance.

This didn't only happen with Judas; God worked this way with all the highlighted characters in the Bible, both in the Old and New Testaments. Even with all their mistakes, God forgave them and drew them to Him. But it doesn't end with them. He continues to work with us, with our secret sins and open rebellion, because He loves us with His everlasting love *(Jeremiah 31:3)* and seeks to draw us closer to Him.

CONCLUSION

God's Call for You

Today, Jesus is presenting you with eternal life and eternal death. Eternal life is given so you can inherit the kingdom of heaven prepared for you from the foundation of the world, and eternal death is prepared for the devil and his angels *(Matthew 25:34, 41)*. I pray that you choose the kingdom of heaven which is prepared for us.

I pray you accept that eternal life. The proof of accepting it is showing everlasting love to others. *1 Corinthians 13:13* reminds us that *"for the greatest of these is LOVE."* This is the only way God can take us to heaven because God doesn't make heaven fit for our convenience; instead, He makes us fit for heaven's principles.

As you see the power and impact of these nine key components for a quality life, I pray that they will bring a revival in your heart and that you may allow God to develop the fruit of the Spirit in you and make you fit for heaven. This is the best quality of life to live, and no matter your circumstances, you can start now!

> *"But the fruit of the Spirit is love, joy, peace, longsuffering, kindness, goodness, faithfulness, gentleness, self-control. Against such there is no law. And those who are Christ's have crucified the flesh with its passions and desires. If we live in the Spirit, let us also walk in the Spirit"* (Galatians 5:22–25).

AMEN!

*I want to take this moment to thank God
for inspiring me to write this book.
Throughout the writing process,
I saw clearly the areas in my life
where I needed to let God work in me.
I learned about God's unblemished character on a deeper level.
This experience brought me closer to God
and sparked a revival within me.
My prayer is that as you read this book,
it will not just be a book to read but an experience of
greater closeness with God like never before,
leading to a revival in your hearts.*

ABOUT THE AUTHOR

Martin Raj has a bachelor's degree in Health Ministry and is a Certified Life and Relationship Coach. He is passionate about traveling, learning, cooking, and wellness. He has worked in various wellness centers worldwide and spearheaded a wellness awareness project in Northern New England. Raised by a single mother, Martin learned from an early age that life is not easy and that hard work is essential. He became the primary caregiver for his mum when she became ill, contuning in that role until she passed away. Through that experience, he developed a deep interest in health, disease, and prevention. Since then, his journey of searching for God, meaning, and purpose led him to his personal encounter with Jesus and to learn how to have a quality life even when all that he treasured is gone. Through privation, dedication, and God's grace, he has gained valuable insights and continues to learn and share practical tips as a Life and Relationship Coach. He loves to challenge people's thinking, put a smile on a stranger's face, and connect with God and others in an authentic, genuine, and profound way. He has resolved never to take anyone or his own life for granted.

Now, as a team with his wife, they are dedicated to their ministry, Natural Healing Project. Their mission is to empower others in their journey of healing relationships with God, oneself, and others by connecting to The Source of love. They focus on developing a secure attachment style, enhancing communication skills, the power of forgiveness, and promoting empowering thoughts. Traveling to various locations, they conduct workshops covering wellness and relationship topics, offer coaching services, and share natural products. Building meaningful connections, ministering together, exploring new places, and forming friendships bring them joy. Their shared passion for wellness and relationships fuels their enthusiasm for their mission, aiming to motivate others on their journey toward health, a positive mindset, and fulfilling relationships.

Join the Healing Journey at
www.NaturalHealingProject.com
Instagram @NaturalHealingProject

GROWING FOR GOD

God said the Fruits of the Spirit do I need, to live
And I want to live right by showing my love,
Living by myself in this world could destroy
But depending on Abba, Father, gives great joy.

Knowing God's love for me will never cease
I want to live this life completely in peace
As He walks me through the fiery suffering
He is simply training me to be long-suffering.

He has saved me through His Son's greatness
Accepting this truth nurtures my gentleness,
When He knocks on my heart with tenderness
I will open it to develop in me His goodness.

When Satan tempts me with his sinful trait
I'll pray to God and walk upright with faith,
God's Word strengthens me during weakness
My fallibility brings me to my knees with meekness.

The most beautiful days are with Jesus' presence
I prepare myself each day with all temperance,
Given guidelines for eternity is simple and straight
Spending eternity with my God is simply great! Amen!

- Martin Raj
03.30.2018

WHAT WE OFFER

Natural Healing Project

RESOURCES
Healing Relationships with God, ourselves and others!

BRING US TO YOUR AREA
Support your team, church, or organization by offering interactive workshops on wellness, healthy living, cooking, fostering empowering thoughts, and cultivating healthy relationships.

Contact us to come to your area!

WELLNESS 1:1 COACHING
As a holistic wellness coach, we aim to empower clients to achieve balance and harmony in all aspects of their lives, fostering a sense of well-being beyond physical health.

Sign-up to become a better you!

RELATIONSHIP 1:1 COACHING
The goal is to help clients develop healthier relationships with themselves, God, and others while dating, with their spouses, and with those around them.

Sign-up to start working on building a healthy relationship.

WELLNESS RESOURCES

Visit our website to find more resources: books, blogs, educational material, and natural products. connect with us via email, social media or our website.

Find us in social media: *@NaturalHealingProject*
email: *Nathealingproject@gmail.com*
Website: *NaturalHealingProject.com*

Made in the USA
Columbia, SC
12 September 2024